Brussels & Antwerp
Eating & Drinking

timeout.com/brussels

Penguin Books

PENGUIN BOOKS

Published by the Penguin Group
Penguin Books Ltd, 80 Strand, London WC2R ORL, England
Penguin Books USA Inc., 375 Hudson Street, New York, New York 10014, USA
Penguin Books Australia Ltd, 250 Camberwell Road, Camberwell, Victoria 3124,
   Australia
Penguin Books Canada Ltd, 10 Alcorn Avenue, Toronto, Ontario, Canada M4V 3B2
Penguin Books (NZ) Ltd, cnr Rosedale and Airborne Roads, Albany, Auckland, New
   Zealand

Penguin Books Ltd, Registered Offices: Harmondsworth, Middlesex, England

First published 2003
10 9 8 7 6 5 4 3 2 1

Copyright © Time Out Group Ltd, 2003
All rights reserved

Colour reprographics by Icon, Crowne House, 56-58 Southwark Street, London
SE1 1UN

Printed and bound by Cayfosa-Quebecor, Ctra. de Caldes, Km 3 08 130 Sta,
Perpètua de Mogoda, Barcelona, Spain

Edited and designed by
Time Out Guides Limited
Universal House
251 Tottenham Court Road
London W1T 7AB
Tel + 44 (0)20 7813 3000
Fax + 44 (0)20 7813 6001
Email guides@timeout.com
www.timeout.com

Editorial

Editor Peterjon Cresswell
Deputy Editor Will Fulford-Jones
Chief Reviewer Gary Hills
Listings Editors Wim Verhaeghe, Yvan Vonck
Maps Editors Gary Hills, Peter Soetens
Proofreader Phil Harriss

Editorial Director Peter Fiennes
Series Editor Sarah Guy
Guides Co-ordinator Anna Norman

Design

Group Art Director John Oakey
Art Director Mandy Martin
Art Editor Scott Moore
Senior Designer Tracey Ridgewell
Picture Editor Kerri Miles
Acting Picture Editor Kit Burnet
Acting Picture Deputy Editor Martha Houghton
PictureTrainee Bella Wood
Scanning & Imaging Dan Conway
Ad make-up Glen Impey

Advertising

Group Commercial Director Lesley Gill
Sales Director Mark Phillips
International Sales Manager Ross Canadé
Advertisement Sales (Brussels & Antwerp) TKR
Advertising Assistant Sabrina Ancilleri

Administration

Chairman Tony Elliott
Chief Operating Officer Kevin Ellis
Managing Director Mike Hardwick
Group Financial Director Richard Waterlow
Group Marketing Director Christine Cort
Marketing Manager Mandy Martinez
US Publicity & Marketing Associate Rosella Albanese
Group General Manager Nichola Coulthard
Guides Production Director Mark Lamond
Production Controller Samantha Furniss
Accountant Sarah Bostock

Contributors

Introductions *Eating in Brussels, The cuisine of Belgium, Eating & drinking in Antwerp* Gary Hills; *Drinking in Brussels, Beers of Belgium* Peterjon Cresswell. **Restaurant & bar reviews** Gary Hills, Peterjon Cresswell and Peter Soetens. **Features** Gary Hills, except: *Cruising for a boozing, A breath of fetid Eire, Inside the Belgian bar, High times in Flanders* Peterjon Cresswell; *Right said Fred* Micha Kapetanovic/Kiosque; *The curse of the gueuze* Jeremy Duns.

The Editor would like to thank Frank Deijnckens at the Antwerp Tourist Office; Dawn Page and all at Tourism Flanders-Brussels; Sue Heady at the Tourist Office of Brussels and Wallonia; Micha Kapetanovic, Katia Serres and all at Kiosque; Erik Stock and the Hasselt Genever Museum. Peter Soetens would like to thank Myriam Kenis and Curt De Laet.

Maps JS Graphics (john@jsgraphics.co.uk).

Photography Sarah Blee, except: pages 13, 16, 61, 119, 150, 153 Hadley Kincade; page 213 Héloïse Bergman.

Contents

Brussels

Antwerp

About the guide

The reviews in this guide are based solely on the experiences of *Time Out* restaurant reviewers. All the restaurants, bars and cafés listed here were visited anonymously over a period of a few months, and *Time Out* footed the bills. No payment of any kind from restaurant owners has secured or influenced a review in this guide.

In the listings, the times given are those observed by the kitchen; in other words, the times within which one is fairly certain to be able to sit down and order a meal. These can change according to time of year and the owners' whims. It is often a good idea to call ahead; pleasingly, staff at most establishments in Brussels and Antwerp speak English. Average prices listed are per person for three courses, excluding drinks and service. Average prices have been graded on the following scale:

up to €20	€
€20 to €30	€€
€30 to €45	€€€
€45 to €60	€€€€
over €60	€€€€€

We list the credit cards accepted by the restaurant or bar by initials: AmEx (American Express), DC (Diners Club), MC (MasterCard) and V (Visa).

The star system is there to help you identify top performers at a glance. A red star – ★ – by the name of a restaurant means that our reviewers found it to be one of the best in the city.

Eating

in Brussels

All Belgians consider themselves food experts. Happily
for the visitor, they're very keen to share their knowledge.
Ask locals for a restaurant recommendation and they'll tap
their nose as if offering a precious secret, but they'll still
cheerily point you in the right direction, content that their
nous proved useful. And in Brussels, there are plenty of
directions in which to point. It is estimated that there are
nearly 2,000 restaurants in a city of a million people. The
whole place could disappear *à table* at any given moment.

Try to grab a seat in any number of popular restaurants
at lunchtime or at weekends, and it's easy to believe it
has. Eating out is a national hobby in Belgium; in Brussels,
it's an everyday occurrence. If you're out and about at
8pm and a restaurant is empty, it's likely to be a duffer.

The best eating experiences are to be found in the
scores of small restaurants: cosy and traditional, lined with
wooden furniture, white-globe lamps and tiled walls and
floors. The food here is pleasingly free of frills. That said,

timeout.com

The online guide to the world's greatest cities

there are also many places here irresistible to gourmands. Fine French cooking is not only admired but encouraged; locals applaud quality and artistry. It helps that Belgium has more Michelin stars per capita than France.

What and where

Whether mussels and chips, fish stews or hulking steaks, traditional Belgian food takes pride of place. Menus tend to reflect a broad range of geographic influences, from the Flemish coast through to Wallonia and the border regions; a waterzooi from Ghent will be found on the same carte as cured ham from the Ardennes. Newer Belgian restaurants, which attract a younger clientele, tend to experiment with the formulas, adding fiddly bits of this and a garnish of that. Yet the basic approach remains the same.

Brussels falls easily into areas, but it's difficult to pigeonhole them with a specific style of eating. Starting with the centre of town, although tourist friendly, the Grand' Place is a decent bet for food, often dished up in traditional eateries. While there are some upmarket joints, you're just as likely to find a bargain as anywhere in the city.

In nearby Sablon, prices are generally more expensive, as they are in St-Gilles and pockets of the vast Ixelles area. It's in these neighbourhoods that you'll find some of the city's more modern Belgian restaurants, which appeal to young diners keen on atmosphere and style as well as food. North of Grand' Place is Ste-Catherine, where the area around the fish market is filled with seafood restaurants. But if you want real Belgian, head for Les Marolles, where the bars and restaurants are heavily slanted to the locals.

It's not all Belgian and French, of course. Brussels' big north African population has introduced the cuisine of Morocco and Tunisia to the city, along with Algerian and Lebanese styles. Head to parvis de St-Gilles to sample some, or journey to the Matongé in Ixelles (see p119 **Do the Congo**) for some Congolese cooking. Less exotically, Spanish, Portuguese, Greek and sub-continental Indian cuisines are well represented, while in St-Géry, you'll find a range of oriental restaurants (see p64 **Chinese whispers**).

How

You won't feel rushed here. A meal in Brussels is
something to be savoured. This is not a city in which you'll
be asked to vacate a table almost before you've put down
your dessert spoon. Such attitudes are reflected in the
service. It'll always be courteous, but – especially in some
of the more traditional places – it may not always be quick.
If you're sitting at a table or at the bar, you'll generally
be expected to run a tab. If you're sat on a terrace, it's
pay-as-you-go. In busier places, waiters have their own
allocated tables, so pay the one from whom you ordered.

You will often see the sign 'snack-resto' in eathouse
windows. This is more to do with style than food: snack-
restos tend to be simply furnished places, with paper
napkins and no tablecloths. Most snack-restos are pop-in,
pop-out places with a fairly high turnover; typical of the
breed is **Da Kao** (*see p64*).

Pubs and bars come with similar categorisations.
The word 'taverne' is used in both French and Flemish to
denote traditional Belgian ale-houses that serve nothing
more to eat than a plate of cheese or a croque-monsieur.

A bar has a slightly more upmarket feel, and is usually a place for bright young things to meet friends, read the papers or do some work.

In general, Belgium is very relaxed about dress codes and most restaurants in this guide are welcoming to all-comers. If an establishment does require a dress code, we've generally mentioned it in the entry, though you'd do well to dress well – and jackets are more important here than ties – for anything in the €€€€€ price bracket. Some trendy places, such as **Belga Queen** (see *p25*), have security on the door, and may not let you in if you're wearing your battered trainers. But such occurences are rare: phone and ask if you're not sure.

When

Lunchtime, known as midi, is busy in Brussels, with most people taking a proper meal break. Service usually starts at noon and goes on until 3pm at the latest. In the evening, restaurants open relatively early: a 6.30pm start is common. Most serve until 10.30pm or 11pm, though some fine-dining restaurants take last orders nearer 9.30pm. Restaurants generally stay open for an extra half-hour on weekends.

That said, there are no hard and fast rules here. Some places close on Sundays and/or Mondays, others stay open seven days a week. As for holidays, Brussels does not shut down in summer in the manner of, say, Paris. Some restaurants will take a short break in July or August; closing for the first two weeks of January is also not uncommon. Restaurants that close on Sundays also usually shut on bank holidays too. But whenever you eat out here, try and book ahead, especially on weekends (lunch and dinner).

Prices and payment

Eating out in Brussels is not particularly cheap. Some restaurants do offer a set menu, more often at lunch than dinner. Look out for the plat du jour, served during the day.

When compared to Britain and the US, wines in Belgian restaurants are reasonably priced. Because the country is not a major producer of wine, you can expect to find a

broad range of bottles and/or glasses on the menu: it's not unusual to find French, Italian, Spanish and New World varieties on the same list. House wine is generally decent.

Service is always included in the total bill and tips are not expected, though people round up the bill as a courtesy. In top restaurants it is usual to leave a little more.

The price guidelines used throughout this book measure the average cost of a starter, main course and dessert without drinks and service. For a full explanation of our price-coding system, *see p2*.

The Cuisine
of Belgium

The Belgians are fond of saying that their food is cooked with French finesse but served in German portions.
You only need to glance at any of Breughel's vivid scenes of peasant banqueting to realise this is no modern phenomenon. Food has been at the heart of this region for centuries, and modern-day recipes have changed little down the years.

In the Middle Ages, what is now Belgium was the centre of northern Europe's spice trade. These spices were used to enliven brewing, and flavours such as ginger, coriander, nutmeg and caraway were incorporated into beers. As these beers were then used for slow-cooking meat, so distinctive flavours to the dishes began to emerge, establishing a style practically unknown to the soft southerners in France.

Yet Belgium has always looked outside its borders to find inspiration for its own cooking, and has never been afraid of borrowing from other sources or cultures. Neighbours Germany, France and the Netherlands, along with nearby Switzerland, have all offered ideas and ingredients over time. But it's simplest to say that Belgian food is a heady mix of proud and traditional home cooking spruced up with some French highlights. The culinary exchange between the two countries continues today, with the pair gently sparring over who has the world's top chefs.

Without doubt, Belgium is a meat and potatoes kind of place. Beef or rabbit cooked in beer is a typical dish, hale and hearty to the last. A traditional restaurant menu will also offer a carbohydrate-heavy range of potato options: croquettes, frites, stuffed baked spuds and half a dozen mashed varieties. Fish and seafood are also popular: prepared simply, they take in cod, sole, mussels, oysters, escargots and the tiny little shrimps, crevettes grises.

However, Belgium is also world renowned for its fine dining. Traditional Belgian recipes play a part, though a French influence can be detected in the popularity of butter-enriched sauces and in ingredients such as truffles and foie gras. Yet even at this highest culinary level, restaurant staff ensure Belgian appetites are sated. At a gastronomic temple such as **Comme Chez Soi** (*see p27*), your main will arrive immaculately presented. But what if you're still hungry once it's all gone? No problem. Over strolls a waiter with a mundane serving dish and fills your plate with seconds. The presentation takes a running jump, but the food is just as stunning as the first time around.

Belgian food unites a country divided by language. Game from the Ardennes forest is served in Antwerp; the Flemish coastline provides tonnes of mussels for Liège. The low-lying fertile soil erupts with potatoes, chicory and, in May and June, fat white asparagus. Great beef tomatoes provide a fruit basket for stuffing with shrimps and mayonnaise. And any left-over vegetables are mashed together to make stoemp: similar to bubble-and-squeak, but served with a thick slice of hot ham or sausage.

Liège is the area from which the boudin sausage hails, either white or black pudding. Delving further into the guts of the matter, andouillette is a rough-cut bladder filled with offal and chitterlings. Its varieties are graded by the number of As after its name; AAAAA varieties are not for the faint-hearted, but you get full marks for effort.

Several dishes are common to the majority of Belgian menus. For example, almost every Belgian restaurant will have fondues au fromage or croquettes aux crevettes

listed as a starter. Both are deep-fried: the first with a gluggy cheese sauce, the second a gluggy pink sauce thick with prawns.

Elsewhere, it's simple stuff. Eels are served in green sauce, herrings are eaten raw and mussels come in a litre pot with a bowl of chips. Steak-frites is endemic, even if it doesn't appear on the menu. Waterzooi is another word you'll see regularly: a thinnish soup-like stew made with river fish or chicken, it has its origins in Ghent. And for dessert? Waffles, chocolate, ginger-cinnamon spéculoos biscuits, spicy pain à la Grecque, and the towering dame blanche, vanilla ice-cream with a hot chocolate sauce.

Once you realise the breadth, depth and quality of Belgian cuisine, you'll want to pick up a library of cookbooks to take home. But when you get around to trying them, don't skimp on the portions. The Belges will never forgive you.

Eating on the hoof

In a city not bothered about time, it's an odd phenomenon. Everyone takes a decent lunch break, and there are cafés, snack-restos and bars on almost every street in town. So why are the Bruxellois happy to walk the streets or ride the métro munching away?

Street food in Brussels has a different feel to it than in other cities. No greasy burger drippings and hot-doggy street-stinks here; the menu tends to be limited to bread, waffles and, at a stretch, breakfast pastries. It's all to do with the democracy of eating in a city that is devoted to the pastime. If you can't sit down to have a decent lunch, then it's socially acceptable to have it on the move – provided you pick from the socially acceptable range of options.

Fast food in Brussels is contained. Ronald McDonald only manages a weak smile here, with one – yes, one – flagship restaurant opposite the Bourse and a couple of others dotted here and there. Brussels, you see, has Quick, a popular Belgian burger chain that taps into the psyche of the locals in a way a McD's never will. It helps that the cones of chips sold at Quick's leave others in the shade.

Frites are a true local glory. The Belgians fry their potatoes twice, once for five minutes at 160°C and then, half an hour later, at 180°C for two minutes. The frites end up golden brown, crispy on the outside and soft in the middle, and come served with an elaborate range of sauces at 6,000 outlets. Brussels' most famous is **Maison Antoine** in place Jourdan, run by the DeSmet family since 1949.

Back at the Bourse, as if in defiance of the flagship McDonald's, the family-run whelk stall **Chez Jef et Fils** has been thriving for over two generations. Considerably more common than whelks are waffles, whether plain, sugared or covered in chocolate; get them from countless outlets.

While fast food is generally socially acceptable, it's not always thus. When the football finishes or the bars start emptying, or even when hordes of teenage tourists descend on the Grand' Place in summer, it all gets messy. Fast-food alley, rue du Marché aux Fromages behind Grand' Place, sinks into a feeding frenzy. Chips become mere embellishment for a wild range of meat-in-baguettes, including boulettes (balls of meat), brochettes (shish kebabs) and the mitraillette, a foot-long baguette stuffed to bursting with hamburger patties, mayonnaise and salad, topped with fries.

As for older folk, the nearest they come to street eating is standing at the whelk booth indulging in a natter and a pot of steaming escargots, or slurping oysters and a glass of Muscadet at the stall on place Ste-Catherine. It's much better for the digestive system.

Drinking

in Brussels

Casual, social or deathwish, drinking in Brussels is invariably a pleasure. The range of bars, the range of beers and the rage of thirst they inspire combine to produce a drinking culture unmatched this side of Berlin. And culture it is, as ritualised as wine-tasting in Burgundy and as traditional as tea-drinking in England.

At the centre of this culture is beer. Not just any old beer, but some 600 varieties in almost as many colours and flavours, brewed by everyone from Trappist monks to major multinational concerns (for some examples, *see p17*). Most bars serve about 20 varieties; others stock 200. They'll be served, with a 's'il vous plaît', in a specially shaped and logoed glass, plonked onto a logoed beermat. Yet despite such ceremony, few bars are pretentious enough to warrant a reciprocal nose-in-the-glass and nod of approval. Sip it, sup it, neck it: simply down the beer as you would anywhere else, before going on to think about the next one.

Do you want to spend some great
time out in Brussels or Antwerp ?

It's all here.

Kiosque, the Brussels monthly events bible, in French.
Kiosk, the Antwerp monthly events bible, in Dutch.

Ask for 'une bière', and you'll get a standard glass of standard draught lager, invariably Maes, Stella or Jupiler and costing €1-€1.50. Request 'une blanche' and you'll find yourself paying €1.50-€2 for a glass of draught wheat beer, almost always Hoegaarden. For a bottle of the more interesting brews, priced €2 and over (for more on these,

see p17), you'll need to ask by name. French speakers should note that asking for a 'demi', as you would do in France, will get you a half-litre and approving nods from your fellow drinkers.

Waiter service is the norm in Brussels; unlike in France, there's no price difference if you sit at the bar, inside or on the terrace. Though some central bars will demand payment for each order, in most spots you'll be expected to pay at the end, and if all you've ordered has been drinks, you need only tip a little, if at all.

Paying extra to drink on the Grand' Place is inevitable, but not budget-busting. That said, many of the cheaper bars nearby are just as historic and ornate; art nouveau, art deco and Surrealism all passed through Brussels, and their instigators enjoyed a drink or two.

Jenever, a pure grain spirit in various fruit flavours, is the national chaser (see p198 **High times in Flanders**). Common brands of whisky and vodka are as ubiquitous as they are in the UK. A Belgian speciality (or peculiarity), especially among the poodle-and-blue-rinse brigade, is half-en-half, usually white wine mixed with champagne. Wine is also readily available by itself in many bars, but it's generally only taken with food.

To help you choose between beers, wines and spirits, most bars will have a drinks menu as comprehensive as their food menu, if not longer. The most modest local

should offer Belgian tapas of salami slices and cheese chunks; the majority of bars reviewed in this book dish up standard Belgian pub grub of stoemp, sausages and stews, plus chips with everything. Coffee comes on a small tray with a little tub of milk and a biscuit. Food is usually served throughout the day; you can dive into almost any corner bar and grab a plate of hot nosh without frills or fuss.

Opening hours here are gloriously lax. Drinking until midnight almost anywhere in town is easy; past 1am, you'll need to be in the centre, where dawn is not an uncommon closing time.

Most visitors to the city are drawn to St-Géry, a small but lucrative scene based around the eponymous square itself, but less formulaic and more fun are the bars down rue du Marché au Charbon (*see p40* **Cruising for a boozing**). If you have only one night in town, drink it here. In Sablon, the bars are as glitzy as those in Les Marolles are authentically scuzzy. Ixelles has a mix of African (rue Longue Vie), trendy (around place St-Boniface), student-oriented (near the cemetery) and snobbish (avenue Louise) bars. Those in St-Gilles have a boho, villagey feel, while the pubs of the EU Quarter provide expats with a drinking and networking facility.

Beers

of Belgium

Beer is Belgium's national treasure. Crafted with love and precision over the centuries, the nation's 600-strong range of brews represents a tradition beyond compare.

Variety is the key here. Offering everything from bog-standard lagers mass-produced by multinationals to finely honed ales brewed by monks to medieval recipes, Belgium is a beer-lover's paradise. Like fine wines, the brewing process can take years. And, as with fine wines, there are strict controls on how any company can describe its brew.

Every bar will stock at least one draught lager, generally Stella, Maes or Jupiler, and a wheat beer, 'une blanche' or a 'witte', usually Hoegaarden but occasionally Brugs or Limburgse. Taste for this cloudy tipple died out after the war, but was revived in the 1990s. Served in tumblers, it's the classic summer drink, thirst-quenchingly quaffable.

A fair number of bars provide a few more adventurous ales on draught ('au fût'/'van't vat'), while a select band of others offer an encyclopaedic range, on tap and from the

Brussels doubts?

Then pick up a copy of this guide

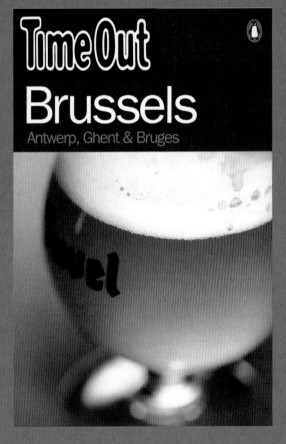

bottle. Of Brussels' bars, **L'Atelier** (*see p119*), **A La Bécasse** (*see p36*), **Le Bier Circus** (*see p82*) and **Chez Moeder Lambic** (*see p134*) offer the most choice; in Antwerp, **Den Engel** (*see p199*) and **Kulminator** (*see p202*) run the gamut of ales from abbey to Westvleteren,

the most obscure of the five breweries officially designated as Trappist.

Many Belgian brews hint at monastic origins, and many were popularised during times of plague. However, only the famous five of Chimay, Orval, Rochefort, Westmalle and Westvleteren have truly been touched by the hand of God. Aside from the dark, unclassifiable Orval, the tricky exception, all are deep brown and creamy; for deep brown and creamy with a kick, select the

dubbel or tripel versions, which deliver up to 9 per cent ABV.

Each Trappist brewery is a working monastery, but few welcome personal visits and sales are strictly controlled. Near each monastery, however (check www.belgium-tourism.net or www.visitflanders.com for directions and details), will be at least one bar and shop happy to flog the stuff. The next ecclesiastical step down are abbey beers such as Leffe and Grimbergen, both frequently spotted on tap due to national distribution deals.

The most unusual family of beers are the lambics, particular to the Brussels area. Lambics are naturally fermented with no added yeast, a process that takes at least a couple of years. A young lambic is called a faro, and quite rare. Indeed, straight lambic is hard to find; it provides the base for two of Belgium's most popular and idiosyncratic, gueuze and fruitlambic. A sometimes painfully acquired taste, gueuze is a delicate mix of young and old lambic (*see p154* **The curse of the gueuze**).

Lambic's very tart taste, however, also makes it the perfect recipient in which to mix small, dark cherries (kriek) and raspberries (framboise or frambozen).

Finally come the hundreds of ales of all colours and for all seasons. Some – particularly brown ales from Oudenaarde, red beers from Rodenbach, strong golden ales such as Duvel and amber De Koninck from Antwerp – are produced by successful provincial breweries. Others – banana beer, anyone? – are obscure almost for the sake of it.

Almost all beers will be served in their own shaped glass, with their own logo and beermat. There's no stigma attached to any variety; you won't be singled out as a bearded obsessive if you order the most obscure one on the menu (and there will be a drinks menu, an extensive one at that). Beer, remember, is a matter of national pride, and drinks are drunk by all: male, female, young and old alike. There are even bières de table for weaning children. Only in Belgium could beer match mother's milk.

Where to...

Grand' Place
& Lower Town

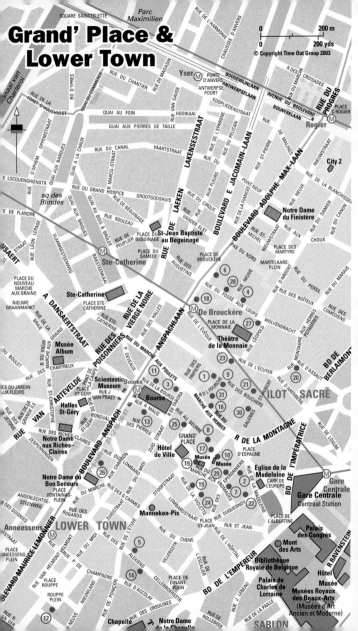

The tiny streets around the Grand' Place, which still follow the city's medieval plan, are alive with restaurants and bars. Surprisingly, their location in the centre of the tourist area doesn't necessarily mean that they are either of poor quality or wildly overpriced. Many of these establishments are used by locals and have a true Belgian feel about them, at least in part because the narrow streets in which they're set are also residential. Restaurants in the area are busy year-round, and it's always best to book ahead if possible.

Restaurants

Belgian & French

Belga Queen

32 rue Fossé aux Loups (02 217 21 87). Métro De Brouckère. **Meals served** noon-2.30pm; 7pm-midnight daily. **Average** €€€€. **Credit** AmEx, DC, MC, V.

The toilets at the Belga Queen have caused enormous controversy. They're unisex, though this is not so unusual in a country where the men's urinal is often situated by the side of the joint-sex hand basins. But these toilets are unisex *and* see-through: the doors to the sit-downs are transparent, though it's up to you to work out the little trick that makes them opaque. Whether or not you manage it, you should find that there are other worthwhile aspects to a meal here. The great vaulted room, with its pillars, deep blue carpets and red chairs, is chic in the extreme. The food is modern Belgian, and, in keeping with the decor, is a little over-designed. That said, the emphasis on fish and the grand oyster bar keeps it anchored to the traditional. Best approached with a group of friends.

Bleu de Toi

73 rue des Alexiens (02 502 43 71). Métro Gare Centrale. **Meals served** noon-2pm, 7.30-11pm Mon-Fri; 7.30-11pm Sat. **Average** €€€. **Credit** AmEx, DC, MC, V.

From the exterior to the calming highlights of the main dining room reflected in the banquettes, water glasses and even wall paintings, a blue theme runs through much of Corine Ceuleman's intimate, relaxed two-floor restaurant, to decadent effect. The buzzier second room, mind, is a spectacular change, all rich reds and purples. The food is brasserie-style cuisine, with bintje (Dutch potatoes) the house speciality; they come with a wide choice of stuffings, among them lobster, smoked salmon, caviar, veal and snails. Desserts include ice-cream with spéculoos (Belgian ginger biscuit) and oriental nougat. Group bookings (for up to 16 people) are available.

Le Cerf

20 Grand' Place (02 511 47 91). Métro Gare Centrale/ Pré-métro Bourse. **Meals served** noon-3pm, 6-11.30pm Mon-Fri. **Average** €€€€. **Credit** AmEx, DC, MC, V.

A trad-look restaurant from the people who brought you Roue d'Or (*see p30*), Le Cerf occupies a narrow house on the corner of Grand' Place. The building's construction date – 1710 – is very much reflected in the interior design: peer through the green-mullioned windows and you might think you're eyeing up a gentlemen's club. Given such history and decor, it comes as no great surprise to find the menu comes with no great surprises: strengths include good fish and lobster, chief among the weaknesses is a total lack of vegetarian options that aren't desserts. Still, while the restaurant's food doesn't live up to its fantastic location – itself made even better if you can blag a window seat – you'll likely leave replete.

Chez Léon

18 rue des Bouchers (02 511 14 15/www.chezleon.be). Métro Gare Centrale/Pré-métro Bourse. **Meals served** 11.30am-11pm daily. **Average** €. **Credit** AmEx, DC, MC, V.

Léon is almost always full to bursting, but rarely with Bruxellois. That's not because the food isn't up to the locals' lofty standards, mind: some of it is. No: it's partly because of its rue des Bouchers location, and partly because this restaurant chain has a brash, bustling, fast-food approach to ambience-creation, when a time-honoured, genteel, dinner-party vibe would go down

Aux Armes de Bruxelles. *See p33.*

better. The photographed menus don't help break the Brussels sneer, but they're handy for kids or the linguistically challenged. The food's basic – mussels, chips, big lumps of meat – but none the worse for it.

Chez Patrick

6 rue des Chapeliers (02 511 98 15). Métro Gare Centrale/Pré-métro Bourse. **Meals served** noon-2.30pm, 6.30-10pm Tue-Sat. **Average** €€. **Credit** AmEx, DC, MC, V.
This homely restaurant just steps from Grand' Place, family run since 1932, had a minor makeover after papa Jean retired around the turn of the century and handed it to his son. Aside from changing its name, Patrick has done a bit of up-marketing, putting maroon tablecloths on the previously papered tables and casing the menus in similarly coloured vinyl covers. Still, most things remain reassuringly the same: the tiled floor, the open cooking range, the theatre posters, the ventilation pipe that goes nowhere. The food, too, is as it ever was, with a menu that takes in a perfect range of Belgian fish and meat dishes, an unrivalled steak in green pepper sauce and what many claim are the best chips in town.

Comme Chez Soi

23 place Rouppe (02 512 29 21). Pré-métro Anneessens. **Meals served** noon-1.30pm, 7-9.15pm Tue-Sat. **Average** €€€€€. **Credit** AmEx, DC, MC, V.

Bier Tempel (56 rue Marché aux Herbes) is, indeed, a temple to the Belgian brew, selling almost every beer made in the country along with the corresponding glasses. Unusual extras include beer jelly for spreading on bread.

CAFE DE BXL

Bar | Brasserie | Restaurant | Salle de banquets

Brasserie ambiance bruxelloise au coeur de la ville,
sur la plus belle place d'Europe
"La Grand'Place to be"

Une vue superbe sur la Grand'Place et l'Hôtel de Ville
Une excellente cuisine avec une touche d'originalité
Un choix privilégié de bières belges
Des cocktails exotiques et branchés
Des gaufres et des crêpes.

Grand'Place 12A | 1000 Brussels | www.cafebxl.be
Tel : +32 2 503 33 25 | Fax : +32 2 503 33 62

Chef Pierre Wynants is one of Europe's top chefs, and his restaurant is in the top stratum of heady haute cuisine. Wynants and his family – wife Marie-Therese is the maître d', son-in-law Lionel Rigolet the second chef – have won every accolade going, including three stars' worth of recognition from the notoriously picky Michelin men and women. The opulence begins the moment you arrive at the door: Comme Chez Soi is set in a grand townhouse with an art nouveau interior. It's amusing to see that old habits die hard: after a beautifully sculpted course arrives at the table, the waiters return with a bowl of seconds, proving that small and immaculate portions just will not do in Belgium. The food, of course, is exceptional, and includes such delights as pigeon stuffed with truffles. The changing set menu can make the bill a bit more bearable.

La Maison du Cygne

2 rue Charles Buls (02 511 82 44). Métro Gare Centrale/ Pré-métro Bourse. **Meals served** noon-2pm, 7-10pm Mon-Fri; 7-10pm Sat. **Average** €€€€€. **Credit** AmEx, DC, MC, V.

There can surely be no grander Brussels building in which to dine. Sitting right on the Grand' Place, this house has associations with Karl Marx, yet it now wafts a distinctly capitalist air across the square: the rich French food, liberally sprinkled with truffles and caviar, costs an arm and a leg. Only those with extremely expansive expense accounts can afford to come here on anything approaching a regular basis, though those without company credit cards can get off a little more lightly by sticking to the set menus (€40-€70). A slightly cheaper bar-restaurant, L'Ommegang, has recently opened in the same building (with the same phone number) for those on the hoof. While the carte remains expensive, a good value lunch menu at €15 is available Mon-Fri.

L'Ogenblik

1 galerie des Princes (02 511 61 51). Métro Gare Centrale. **Meals served** noon-2.30pm, 7pm-midnight Mon-Thur; noon-2.30pm, 7pm-12.30am Fri, Sat. **Average** €€€€€. **Credit** AmEx, DC, MC, V.

Set in the glamorous covered galleries, L'Ogenblik is one of the trendiest places to eat, and to be seen, in Brussels. The interior is nothing exciting – the look is that of an old brasserie with Conran highlights – but the French food is of gastronomic quality. That said, you'll pay for the privilege: the restaurant lives up to its name by emptying your wallet in the blink of an eye. Among the options are an exquisite marmite of fish, a sort of creamy bouillabaisse, and a chateaubriand with goose liver, cooked in a pastry case. Desserts are pricey but irresistible. It's a cosy place, so booking is essential. Oh, and look out for madame who

If you want your chocolate a little livelier in design, try **Brussels Pralines** (4 rue de la Colline), where you can get decent choccies in the shape of cars, aeroplanes and even the Mannequin Pis.

takes the bookings and prepares the bills: she sits at a vast till with a little wooden foot-stool, wearing half-moon glasses and a don't-mess-with-me expression. Classic.

Les 4 Saisons ★

Royal Windsor Hotel, 2 rue de l'Homme Chrétien (02 505 51 00). Métro Gare Centrale. **Meals served** noon-2.30pm, 7-10.30pm Mon-Fri. **Average** €€€€. **Credit** AmEx, DC, MC, V.

As the flagship restaurant of the Hotel Royal Windsor, the 4 Saisons has established itself as a big player in Brussels dining circles down the years, both with hotel guests and well-heeled Belgians. The restaurant – which has its own entrance – is elegant and luxurious, with the stained-glass panels making it easy to forget you're in a modern hotel building. Yet while it's become a favourite venue for quiet business lunches, it's no mere corporate fix. The menu is relatively affordable and nicely structured, and the French cooking is of the highest quality: original creations on the menu include fillet of lamb gratinéed with Corsican brebis cheese.

Roue d'Or ★

26 rue des Chapeliers (02 514 25 54). Pré-métro Bourse. **Meals served** noon-12.30am daily. **Average** €€. **Credit** AmEx, DC, MC, V.

Sacré bleu!

Walking along the restaurant-packed rue de Bouchers and its Petite brother that stretches off it, you'd be forgiven for believing it's been like this since the days of Charlemagne. The impression will be magnified when you take a look behind the menu boards and icy displays of seafood and see the old brick and mullioned windows of the 17th-century houses. The gabled beauties have always been here, of course; however, the present character of the area was only created in 1960, in a rare piece of city planning that was, for its time, quite magnificently progressive.

Officials decided that various narrow streets should be bulldozed to ease the flow of traffic around the Grand' Place. However, after a furious urban uprising from disgruntled residents and shopkeepers understandably unwilling to see their livelihoods crumble to dust, the plan was shelved. Instead, the city elders decided to create untouchable 'islets', small pockets of preserved streets that would continue to form the backbone of the modern Brussels.

A tidy quadrangle of streets north of Grand' Place and framed by rue du Marché aux Herbes, rue de la Fourche, rue

Despite being located just a minute or so from the Grand' Place and all its attendant tourist haunts, this brasserie has won the hearts of Belgians for its authentic food and authentic prices. The menu is fish- and meat-heavy: lamb's tongue, pig's trotter and chitterling sausage sit comfortably with oysters and finely prepared fish (vegetarians shouldn't even bother showing up). The Magritte-inspired decor takes in bowler hats, marble tables, a fountain of flowers and, in the middle of the floor, an outlandish dessert display.

't Kelderke

15 Grand' Place (02 513 73 44). Métro Gare Centrale/ Pré-métro Bourse. **Meals served** noon-2pm daily. **Average** €. **Credit** AmEx, DC, MC, V.
From the outside, you could be forgiven for believing that this is a basement drinking den: as you descend from the square, you might expect to hear the indistinct thump of a well-charged jukebox echoing up the stone steps. Instead, you'll find a hefty throng of hefty locals tucking into hefty plates of hefty Belgian food. It's a buzzy place, conversation and smoke hanging in the air, and cosy too: you may end up brushing elbows with your neighbours. But no matter: this is good, honest Belgian fare at good, honest prices, and bang in the centre of town at that.

de l'Ecuyer and galeries St-Hubert was the first to be earmarked for such status, earning the name Ilot Sacré 1 in the process. Today, Ilot Sacré is a free *commune*, with its own Burgomaster.

Many of its dignitaries dine in **Aux Armes de Bruxelles** (*see p33*), one of over 45 restaurants and bars that line the cobbled, pedestrianised streets and have brought tourists and revenue to a previously run-down area. The Bouchers are packed with restaurants of every stripe, from seafood eateries with outlandish displays to Italian, Greek, Chinese and beyond.

The atmosphere here is lively, especially in the summer when the terraces fill with diners and drinkers. Barkers stand on the street enticing you in; stalls sell jewellery and souvenirs, a gallery hawks garish art; neon lights guide the way, street-side menus blaring out their bargain meals.

But try not to be sucked in too far. You will see few locals eating here, for the food is generally average and the prices are not quite as enticing as they seem at first glance. But take a slow walk, make a considered decision and go for it. If the food disappoints, the atmosphere won't.

MEZZO

PLACE SAINT GÉRY / SINT GORIKSPLEIN - 18 BORGVAL
B- BRUSSEL 1000 BRUXELLES
TÉL: +32 2 647 66 50 - Fax: +32 2 646 53 94
WWW.MEZZO.BE - INFO@MEZZO.BE

La Taverne du Passage

30 galerie de la Reine (02 512 37 32/
www.tavernedupassage.com). Métro Gare Centrale.
Meals served noon-midnight daily. **Average** €€€.
Credit AmEx, DC, MC, V.

A veritable time-machine of a restaurant, this, a perfectly preserved 1920s eatery where white-jacketed, gold-epauletted waiters serve traditional Belgian food with a traditional and efficient brusqueness in a red room. It's all very yes-sir-no-sir, but come away with the distinct impression that the retainers hobble off for a rest between courses. All the classic dishes are here – mussels, of course, and kidneys in mustard sauce – and if you want to try a slice of real Bruxelloise dining, this is the place to come. The restaurant's location in the covered galleries means you're always protected from the rain on the outside terrace.

Fish & seafood

Aux Armes de Bruxelles ★

13 rue des Bouchers (02 511 21 18/www.armebrux.be).
Métro Gare Centrale. **Meals served** noon-11.15pm
Tue-Sun. **Average** €€€. **Credit** AmEx, DC, MC, V.

Sitting rather grandly in the virtual theme park of fish restaurants near the Grand' Place, Aux Armes is a Brussels institution beloved by local businessfolk and middle-aged, middle-class Belgians. The art deco interior is absolutely authentic, as are the art deco waiters; you'll pay a little more here, but it's probably worth it for the quality of the food you'll be eating and the slice of the good life you'll be living. There's a wide range of classics on the menu (and on the set menus, priced €28.50-€33), but Aux Armes is particularly renowned for its perfect mussels and chips. It's also packed every night, and booking is essential.

Restaurant Vincent

8-10 rue des Dominicains (02 511 26 07/
www.restaurantvincent.com). Métro De Brouckère.
Meals served noon-2.45pm, 6.30-11.30pm Mon-Fri;
noon-3pm, 6.30-10.30pm Sat, Sun. **Average** €€.
Credit AmEx, DC, MC, V.

The rule? Avoid the formulaic restaurants in the rue des Bouchers area. The exception? Vincent, founded in 1905. You make your entrance, uniquely, through the bustling kitchen, and the exquisitely tiled main room is crammed with tables shaped like fishing smacks. Yet this is no theme restaurant: the menu is serious stuff and the restaurant as close as you're likely to get to a traditional Bruxelloise experience. Food includes a fine selection of raw seafood including oysters and mussels, lobster in a

Experience Brussels as it was almost 200 years ago by walking into **Dandoy** (31 rue au Beurre), a perfect time capsule selling home-made marzipan, speculoos biscuits and the spicy bread pain à la grecque.

Restaurant Vincent.
See p33.

number of varieties, and sole fillets wrapped around a mousseline of crayfish. Meat and offal also feature heavily, with slabs of steak and perfect pink kidneys in mustard. A tiny warning: the set menu may seem enticing price-wise, but it's a little unadventurous and tired. If you can, go with the main carte. Whichever you choose, the brigade of waiters – all men, all white with gold braiding – will treat you with professional respect.

Sea Grill

Radisson SAS Hotel, 47 rue du Fossé aux Loups (02 227 31 20). Métro De Brouckère. **Meals served** noon-2pm, 7-10pm Mon-Fri. **Average** €€€€. **Credit** AmEx, DC, MC, V.
Sea Grill is regarded by many as the top seafood restaurant in Belgium. Certainly, chef Yves Mattagne has won a chestful of gongs for his innovative style, based on traditional French preparation yet utterly modern with it. The restaurant is buried deep inside a five-star hotel, and the approach to it is rather corporate. Once inside, however, you'll be seated in pure luxury, surrounded by specially commissioned etched glass fjords. Look out for the 40-kilo lobster press designed by Christoffle, one of three in the world. Watching it in action may make you decide to have the bisque. Or not. Set menus run from €49 to €72.

International

Al Barmaki

67 rue des Eperonniers (02 513 08 34). Métro Gare Centrale. **Meals served** 7pm-midnight Mon-Sat. **Average** €€. **Credit** AmEx, DC, MC, V.

This Lebanese restaurant, near the Grand' Place, sits on a distinctive little street full of tattoo parlours and new-world jewellery shops. The restaurant offers the usual Middle Eastern staples – kebabs, falafel, houmous, tabouleh – and is great for vegetarians or those who are stuffed to bursting with Belgian meats. The Kalach family, who have been here for 30 years, encourage you to eat with your fingers, though they'll get very greasy as you work your way through the meze, fried aubergine, little kebabs and vine leaves stuffed with rice and spices. Great bowls of salad with peppers and cucumbers keep you on your toes; in general, though, portions are huge and prices are cheap.

La Cave de Yasmina

9 rue Marché aux Fromages (02 512 83 40). Métro Gare Centrale. **Meals served** 11am-6pm daily. **Average €. No credit cards**.
You may need to don sunglasses before a walk along Brussels' very own little Latin quarter, crammed into a semi-pedestrianised street behind the Grand' Place. Garish neon, loud music and door-to-door kebab and chip shop fronts all meld into one, though out of them all, friendly Yasmina's is probably the best. The menu here is slightly more sophisticated than those of its neighbours: while the rest of the restaurants on the street deal chiefly in burning racks of lamb dripping, Yasmina's also offers a light vegetarian kebab.

Rugantino

184-6 boulevard Anspach (02 511 21 95). Pré-métro Bourse. **Meals served** noon-3pm, 6.30pm-midnight Mon-Fri; 6.30pm-midnight Sat. **Average €€**. **Credit** AmEx, DC, MC, V.
An art deco emporium of traditional Italian food, right in the centre of Brussels' nightlife district. The menu is decidedly safe – pastas, pizzas (authentically made in a wood-burning stove) and meats – but it's the kind of place you visit because you know exactly what you want and precisely what you'll get. Rugantino is a no-nonsense place that fills to the brim in the early evenings with bright young things meeting up before going on to bright young places, yet at other times, it becomes a quieter family restaurant with an almost serene formality. Take your pick.

Samourai

28 rue du Fossé aux Loups (02 217 56 39). Métro De Brouckère. **Meals served** noon-2pm, 7-9pm Mon, Wed-Sat; 7-9pm Sun. **Average €€€€. Credit** AmEx, DC, MC, V.
It's not easy to find this place: it's tucked away in a quiet arcade, and given the number of old travel posters plastered over the walls of the tiny first room (which also

Oliviers & Co (28 rue au Beurre) sells a fantastic range of Mediterranean olive oils and associated gadgets. When asked if it's a gift, always say yes, and take away your buys in a neat brown bag with a punched metal tag.

contains a bar), you'd be forgiven for thinking you'd walked into a travel agency. From this entrance, small stairs lead up through a labyrinth of rooms. And the food? You won't find much better, with fully trained Japanese chefs doing your bidding on the sushi and sashimi. Indeed, the place is so renowned that Japanese tourists come here by the busload not because they miss home cooking, but because the Samourai's reputation has travelled all the way to Japan. The wines are extremely expensive, so stick to the saki.

Tai Hon

45 rue des Eperonniers/35 rue du Marché aux Fromages (02 514 50 58). Métro Gare Centrale.
Meals served 11.30am-3pm, 6-9.30pm daily.
Average €€€. **Credit** AmEx, DC, MC, V.
Two restaurants sharing the same menu, differentiated only by their decor. The one on Eperonniers is a fairly simple and plain affair, while the newer outpost on the corner of Fromages is more modern minimalist, with blacks contrasting with a red brick basis. Owner Ho Chang Ceu is Taiwanese, and his kitchen specialises in Taiwanese food with a Japanese twist. It's finely executed stuff, fresh and delicate: we can recommend the San Pei chicken, made with soy, sesame oil and saki and spiced up with chilli pepper. The Japanese influence also extends to the pickled dishes, which include vegetables eaten not only raw, but used to enhance the cooking pot. If you've never tried Taiwanese food before, this is a great place to start. You're in Brussels, after all…

Bars

A La Bécasse

11 rue de Tabora (02 511 00 06). Pré-métro Bourse.
Open 10am-1am Mon-Sat; 10am-midnight Sun.
Credit MC, V.
Bundling down a doorway after a bird and a red 'Come and get it, folks' neon arrow would spell Dodge City in other downtown areas, but here the bird is of brass carved into the pavement, the doorway is beautifully tiled, and the bar's interior whispers gravitas. Not of the Gothic era, which saw the rebuilding of the Grand' Place and its taverns after the French bombardment of 1695, but – according to the plaque over the ornate door – dating back to 1877, if not earlier. The Woodcock does at least boast big jugs, filled with draught ales; among them are the rare lambic doux, made according to a tradition long pre-dating Marshal de Villeroy's destruction of medieval Brussels.

Café Métropole

31 place de Brouckère (02 219 23 84). Métro/Pré-métro De Brouckère. **Open** 9am-1am daily. **No credit cards**.
Built in 1900 (five years after the adjoining hotel of the same name), this grande dame has seen stars of the silent, talking and TV eras pass through its gilded, chandelier-sparkled interiors. It was built by the Wielemann brewing dynasty, when Brussels was awash with money and local architects were happy to spend other people's on brash ornamentation. The hotel has been living off its legend a tad too long, but the café has never failed to show the right profile: the delicate ironwork, mirrored walls and ritzy upholstery ooze class. It's not cheap, but for a few Euros more, you could get into character and order a dish of caviar. The terrace tables overlook downtown traffic.

Le Cirio

20 rue de la Bourse (02 512 13 95). Pré-métro Bourse. **Open** 10am-late daily. **No credit cards**.
A classically authentic downtown bar, Le Cirio is named after the famous Italian grocer who shipped wagons of meats, sauces and cheeses over the Alps from Turin to his ornate delicatessen by the stock exchange. Both Bourse and deli have since folded, but the ornamentation remains: beautiful fittings and Vermouth promotions, cash registers and century-old gastronomy awards, and the still-popular half-en-half wine (half sparkling, half still, wholly Italian). Grandes dames and their lookalike poodles sip away the afternoon, the former from a stemmed glass, the latter from a bowl of tap water. Pre-war toilets complete the experience.

Falstaff

19-25 rue Henri Maus (02 511 87 89). Pré-métro Bourse. **Open** 11am-1am daily. **Credit** AmEx, DC, MC, V.
Probably the most famous bar in Brussels, and certainly the most evergreen. An awning on one side of the Bourse barely prepares the first-time visitor for the eye candy of the art nouveau interior, which has been attracting Bruxellois of every stripe for the better part of a century. It's a restaurant, too, but the reasonably priced mains are but a side dish to the range of beers and generous hours: a rare and delicious brew served in elegant surroundings after midnight, a mere step from the town's main square, is more than most European capitals can dream about.

La Fleur en Papier Doré

55 rue des Alexiens (02 511 16 59). Pré-métro Anneessens. **Open** 11am-1am Mon-Thur, Sun; 11am-3am Fri, Sat. **No credit cards**.

What Londoners take when they go out.

Time Out
London

EVERY WEEK

As the favoured haunt of the Surrealists, this quirky establishment would make a mint from the tourist trail were it not stuck on one of those obscure grey steep streets whose only function is to connect the Lower and Upper Towns. It's not that La Fleur is far from the action: it's just the wrong side of a pleasant stroll for what is effectively the *Antiques Roadshow* with obscure artistic pedigree. La Fleur attracts the more unusual tourist, happy to gawp at the doodles and sketches and stagger around in Magritte's wonky footsteps. An artistically active bunch of regulars, albeit a modest one, alleviate their solitude.

Goupil Le Fol

22 rue de la Violette (02 511 13 96). Métro Gare Centrale. **Open** 7pm-5am daily. **No credit cards**.
Sometime in the '70s, Goupil decided to change the world with 'togetherness, music and fruit wine'. He filled this obscure cavern with intimate booths, several suitcases of 45s, beads, neon and other accoutrements, doused the whole lot in penny-chew coloured wines, lit it up, hiked the prices, then stood back and retired laughing, letting pretty bar girls fill in the gaps untouched by the ambience. Kitsch, gimmicky but somehow irresistible, Goupil is the ideal spot to up the ante if the evening is moving from mere acquaintance to something a little more carnal.

L'Imaige de Nostre Dame

8 rue du Marché aux Herbes (02 219 42 49). Pré-métro Bourse. **Open** noon-midnight Mon-Thur; noon-12.30am Fri; 2.30pm-1am Sat; 4pm-midnight Sun. **Credit** AmEx, MC, V.
Of the same character as A La Bécasse – in fact, of the same management – Nostre Dame plays the heritage card with the requisite aplomb, an old wooden tavern tucked down a hidden alleyway downtown. Once inside, long wooden benches offset the assorted neo-medieval tat, and hulking plates of meat-heavy dishes suggest being placed royally back into the 16th century. If ever a PR company were to relaunch mead as a modern drink *du choix*, they'd do so here. In their absence, though, a comprehensive menu of beers entices the visitor to stay just that little bit longer.

La Lunette

3 place de la Monnaie (02 218 03 78). Métro/Pré-métro De Brouckère. **Open** 9am-1am Mon-Thur; 9am-2am Fri, Sat; 10am-1am Sun. **No credit cards**.
A two-floor interior of curved green benches may tempt the odd passer-by to this busy shopping junction behind De Brouckère, but bloody great buckets of beer ('lunettes') primitively scrawled on boards outside grab you by your lapels and drag you in. Eight varieties on tap spoil you for choice, but your pick will invariably be complimented

by the knowing wait staff. The key to La Lunette is time. In England, a skip full of beery would be downed in one, and a third ordered while draining the second in case supplies ran dry or the bell rang. Here, shoppers, office workers and cinemagoers are free to linger and enjoy.

A La Mort Subite

7 rue des Montagnes aux Herbes Potagères (02 513 13 18). Métro Gare Centrale. **Open** 11am-1am Mon-Sat; 1pm-1am Sun. **Credit** MC, V.

Plus belge, tu meurs. Named after a card game and a variety of fruit beer whose hangovers easily assume the literal mantle of Sudden Death, the popularity of this classically dissolute café soon saw the name pass into legend. Earning such post-booze pain is a real pleasure in this narrow, wood-and-mirrored haven of ensozzlement, thick with tobacco smoke and rife with bar tales. You could write your lifework novel before any of

Cruising for a boozing

Most guidebooks direct the unversed and thirsty Brussels visitor to St-Géry. Congregated around this former covered market is a gaggle of sleek, bright bars, each with a catchy little name – but few have any character to match. You will get drunk, certainly, but you will be bored. No, for the discerning drinker with only one night of leave on Brussels' beery shores, there is but one option: rue du Marché au Charbon.

A crawling king snake of a street sliding south-west of Grand' Place, Charbon begins as a mere tributary of the great square, its focal role in the local gay community delineated by small rainbow-flagged bars and businesses clustered at its apex. The most famous is **Le Belgica** (No.32, no phone, http://lebelgica.be), a destination bar where gays of both sexes collide and collude.

Cross the main rue de Lombard and you will immediately be bombarded by bar signs, enticed by neon and spoilt for choice within a remarkably short stretch of atmospheric sidewalk. The narrow street is lined with old style townhouses, many converted into bars, most of a convivial gay/straight mix, some with DJs and modest dancefloors. Since the sad demise of Sonik at No.112, few are out-and-out nightclubs demanding a cover charge.

Standing guard at the gates into barhop heaven is the seminal **Plattesteen** (No.41, 02 512 82 03), a spacious brasserie of exquisite tradition. On the gay circuit without hammering home the point, the Plattesteen can provide ample mozzarella, tomato and basil salads while allowing beer-swillers to pound the pinball

Au Soleil.
See below.

tables awash with reflected neon. A couple of beers to the good, pass on to the **Canoa Quebrada** (No.53, 02 511 13 54), a mysteriously dark bar incongruously lit for the bright salsa and samba sounds on offer. Adjoining the Canoa Quebrada, down a lovely Gothic arched tunnel, festers the primordial bog of the **Rock Classic** bar (No.55, 02 512 15 47), a dark neolithic haven for Van Halen singalongs. Charbon, as we shall see, is a broad church.

Opposite here stands one of the street's biggest draws, the ever popular **Pablo Disco Bar** (No. 60, 02 514 51 49), a small, stylish DJ haunt where the drinks of choice are shaker-served cocktails accompanied by shot glasses.

Latin bars line your path onwards: the old-style tapas bar of **La Guantanameca**

(No.57, no phone), the gaudy **Cartagena** (No.70, 02 502 59 08) and the **Da Caro** (No. 72, no phone), with its colourful cocktails and retro decor.

The best is left for last. Facing each other, by the atmospheric 17th-century church Notre Dame de Bon Secours, are two of the finest examples of modern Brussels bar culture: **Au Soleil** (No.86, 02 513 34 30), a buzzing bohemian spot set in an extravagant old tailor's; and **Fontainas** (No.91, no phone), a delightful retro creation of globe lights, beaded curtains, houseplants and institutional furniture. Invariably excellent music (with DJs on occasions) is complemented by a drinks menu boasting Orval, Vedett and Maredsous brews, and cocktails including the house special of vodka, grapefruit and crème de fraise.

Grand' Place & Lower Town

Le Roy d'Espagne

of the waiters deign to serve you – in fact, attempting to do so would fail to raise many eyelids – but it's all part of the character.

Le Roy d'Espagne

1 Grand' Place (02 513 08 07). Métro Gare Centrale/ Pré-métro Bourse. **Open** 10am-1am daily. **Credit** AmEx, DC, MC, V.

The king of the guildhouses on the gilded square, Le Roy is a classic spot in a prime location, taking full advantage of the tourist trade by filling its warren of dark rooms and corners with dangling marionettes, old prints and pigs' bladders. Don't pity the poor pigs: it's the waiters in monk outfits for whom you should be feeling sorry, as they struggle to keep tabs on dozens of busy tables while tourists scrap it out for one with that view over the Grand' Place.

Toone

21 petite rue des Bouchers (02 513 54 86). Pré-métro Bourse. **Open** noon-midnight daily. **No credit cards**.

This might be a well-known spot on the tourist trail, but to call it a trap would be doing the Toone family a great injustice. Seven generations have worked the local-language puppet theatre here, where the local language is the Bruxellois dialect. This cosy two-room dark-wood establishment is the theatre bar, a familiar stop for many Brussophiles as it's quirky enough to show off to first-time visitors (dangling marionettes and alike), quiet enough to enjoy in whispered intimacy, and not too quaint to put you off coming again. It's signposted from alongside the Musée de la Ville de Bruxelles on the Grand' Place, in case you get confused the next time.

Ste-Catherine

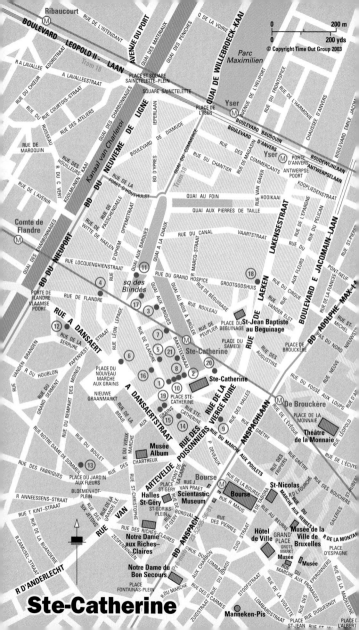

Ste-Catherine

MAP KEY

1. L'Achepot *p45*
2. La Belle Maraichère *p48*
3. Bij den Boer *p51*
4. Chez Martine *p55*
5. Domaine de Lintillac *p46*
6. Gazebo *p54*
7. Jacques *p51*
8. Le Jardin de Catherine *p51*
9. Kafka *p56*
10. I Latini *p54*
11. Le Loup-Galant *p53*
12. Da Mimmo *p54*
13. Le Manufacture *p47*
14. Monk *p56*
15. Le Paon Royal *p47*
16. Le Pré Salé *p47*
17. Strofilia *p55*
18. La Tentation *p56*
19. La Villette *p48*
20. Le Vismet *p53*
21. Le Vistro *p53*

Ste-Catherine

Ste-Catherine was originally filled with canals, on which fishing boats once trawled for goodies. The canals have long since been covered over, but they still lend a special atmosphere to what is now the main dining area in Brussels for lovers of fish and seafood. The restaurants around here are mostly clustered along place Ste-Catherine and the old quays, and many set up canopied terraces in the summer. It's also a good place to buy fish, seafood and other specialist luxury food products. The neighbourhood really comes into its own after dark, as the streets become drenched in neon lights and musicians pipe up to entertain diners and passers-by.

Restaurants

Belgian & French

L'Achepot

1 place Ste-Catherine (02 511 62 21). Métro Ste-Catherine. **Meals served** noon-2.30pm, 6.30-10.30pm Mon-Thur, Sun; noon-2.30pm, 6.30-10.45pm Fri, Sat. **Average** €€. **Credit** MC, V.

Located right in the centre of the Ste-Catherine area, this little restaurant serves up a goodly selection of Belgian favourites and pastas. It's fine for most tastes and leanings, with dishes that range from vegetarian spaghettis to barely cooked lamb's kidneys in mustard sauce. The front room is tiny and crushed, the back room bigger and darkly atmospheric, and the terrace at the front a treat in summer. A great place for lunch.

L'Achepot.
See p45.

Domaine de Lintillac

25 rue de Flandre (02 511 51 23). Métro Ste-Catherine.
Meals served noon-2pm, 7.30-10pm Mon-Fri. **Average**
€. **No credit cards.**

Yes, those are electric toasters set down on each table. And yes, they are there for a reason: you get to do your own brioche to go with your order of pâté de foie gras. And yes, that's foie gras: don't even bother coming here if you're squeamish about meat and/or unsuitable husbandry. This boutique/restaurant is an extension of owner Jean Guillot's farm in the Périgord region of France and is heavy on his duck and goose products, all of which have been overfed and plumped up. The food's remarkably good value, which might explain the need to book your little corner of south-west France at least a week ahead. If you're not quick enough off the mark, you can buy tins of the preserved beasts from the well-stocked shelves.

Champigros
(22 rue Melsens) is a tiny stall selling French wild mushrooms, from spiny chanterelles to chunky boletus, plus fresh herbs, truffles and wild garlic.

Le Manufacture ★

12-20 rue Notre Dame du Sommeil (02 502 26 25).
Métro Ste-Catherine. **Meals served** noon-2pm, 7pm-
midnight Mon-Fri; 7pm-midnight Sat. **Average** €€€€.
Credit AmEx, DC, MC, V.

Brussels folk are used to the fact that some of the
smartest places in town sit in the least likely location.
Take Le Manufacture for one, an old factory nestling
up to a rambling concrete social housing complex. Not
that you can actually see the restaurant from the street,
mind: you'll need to walk through the big gates, then on
through a pretty Japanese-inspired garden, before
you reach this vast and thoroughly modish space. The
food? Modern French/world fusion cooking at its best.
On our most recent visit, we had a cappuccino of wild
mushrooms, pheasant mousse in profiteroles, and an
outrageous combination of scallops and langoustine tails
with Italian egg tomatoes in puff pastry on a choron
sauce. It's not cheap, but the fantastic two-course lunch
menu (€13), which changes daily, is a good way of
introducing yourself to this stunner.

Le Paon Royal

6 rue du Vieux Marché aux Grains (02 513 08 68). Métro
Ste-Catherine. **Meals served** 11.30am-2.30pm, 6-9.30pm
Tue-Sat. **Average** €€. **Credit** AmEx, DC, MC, V.

The Royal Peacock has, it seems, been fanning its
tail-feathers forever. Very proud of itself it is, too,
whether it's serving early-morning breakfasts to a wide
assortment of regulars, or after-dark snacks to evening
revellers. You can come here solely to sup on a beer or a
coffee, but the main menu is definitely well worth
investigating. Fish and seafood feature heavily on it, as
do great slabs of steak served on wooden boards, but
more delicate options (duck breasts, pink kidneys) offer
balance, and there are even decent vegetarian options
(truffle ravioli with fresh tomato, a more predictable
market salad). The customers are a broad cross-section
of inner-city life, so slip in and become one of them.

Le Pré Salé

20 rue de Flandre (02 513 65 45). Métro Ste-Catherine.
Meals served noon-2.30pm, 6.30-10.30pm Wed-Sun.
Average €€€. **Credit** AmEx, MC, V.

A dedicated crowd of (mainly Belgian) diners come to this
family-run restaurant on rue de Flandre for fresh fish,
golden mussels and blummin' great big chunks of meat.
The white-tiled dining room leads directly through to the
open kitchen, where you can see madame preparing your
food to order. It gets pretty packed at times, but the
atmosphere is invariably great, largely due to the top-
notch attitude of the staff: they seem to know everyone.

Friday nights become a bit of a party once the food is finished, with staff joining their customers and friends for a French *chanson* or *deux*, some holiday-camp entertainment and a bit of '70s disco.

La Villette

3 rue du Vieux Marché aux Grains (02 512 75 50).
Métro Ste-Catherine. **Meals served** noon-2.30pm,
6.30-10.30pm Mon-Thur; noon-2.30pm, 6.30-11.30pm
Fri; 6.30-11.30pm Sat. **Average** €€€. **Credit** AmEx,
MC, V.

Quaint, this. Think Swiss chalet, think doll's house, think gingham. Lots of gingham. Red and white checked material figures heavily in the decor of this small restaurant, where the furnishings are as traditional as the Belgian food: uncompromising meat, fish, sausage and game, rich sauces and bubbling casseroles. It's the perfect place to sample some true Belgian cuisine, at least if you and your wallet watch out carefully for the pricey wines. If you feel checkmated by your surroundings, come in summer and sit out on the terrace.

Fish & seafood

La Belle Maraichère ★

11 place Ste-Catherine (02 512 97 59). Métro Ste-Catherine. **Meals served** noon-2.30pm, 6-9.30pm Mon, Tue, Fri-Sun. **Average** €€€. **Credit** AmEx, DC, MC, V.

The self-service salad and pizza bar run by **I Latini** (*see p54*) is perfect for a speedy snack.

Out to dinner

It's nice enough year-round, truth be told. But like many corners of Brussels, Ste-Catherine is at its finest in summer, when diners and drinkers spill out on to the streets and make the most of what decent weather there is.

The old fish-market site, the quai aux Briques, offers the most formal alfresco dining in the area, a swathe of top-end restaurants pulling down stripy awnings. Waiters swing between the traffic and negotiate the cobbles, precariously balancing plateaux de fruits de mer as they run between terrace and kitchen. Above it all sits the floodlit church of Ste-Catherine, spreading her skirts and smiling gently at the madness.

At the front of the church, on place Ste-Catherine, the blaze of restaurants along its side set up a running gauntlet of narrow duck-board terracing, where folk squeeze in with elbows tucked. This is democratic eating, with little fuss or pretension, but a heady buzz wins through as long as you don't mind wandering tourists slowing

Domaine de Lintillac.
See p46.

Madame, Monsieur,
Si la personne qui vous
sert ne vous fait pas
goûter le vin, c'est pour
avoir plus de temps pour
vous sourire!
N'hésitez pas à faire
changer une bouteille
bouchonnée   Merci
            Jean Guillot

NEUFUNK

Ste-Catherine

down their crocodile to ogle your plate on passing.

Further along is Ste-Catherine's most relaxed and informal spot. The Vieux Marché aux Grains, recently renovated and replanted, becomes a mass of plastic tables and chairs in summer. A cross-section gathers: trendies from De Markten, traditionals diving into a beef-in-beer stew at **La Villette** (*see p48*), extended families enjoying a Leffe. Kids run freely, their parents keeping an eye out for the traffic, as buskers try to

earn a bob for a job averagely done (from time to time, stages are set up to allow licensed bands to play late).

Through the chaos sweep flower-sellers, pushing anything from a single rose to a basket bunch in an effort to make your evening a romantic one. A polite but firm 'merci' will send them on their way, but won't stop their competition approaching you moments later. That said, some diners simply can't resist adding that final flourish to a warm and eventful evening under the stars.

LA TENTATION

The green and red-striped **oyster stall** on place Ste-Catherine is open Tue-Sat. Stand and eat a plate of Creuses with a glass of Muscadet or take away ready-opened oysters in seaweed-packed containers.

One of the old quartier classics, this old-fashioned restaurant feels ever so slightly English. It's run by magnificently monikered brothers Freddy and Eddy Devreker, who are both proudly revealed as official Master Chefs of Belgium by the plaques near the front door. If it's tradition you want, this is the place to come: from decor to service, there's only the slightest nod to modern trends. Do try the exquisite marmite des pêcheurs, a pot of fish stew packed with flavour and goodness.

Bij den Boer

60 quai aux Briques (02 512 61 22). Métro Ste-Catherine. **Meals served** noon-2.30pm, 6-10.30pm Mon-Sat. **Average** €€€. **Credit** AmEx, DC, MC, V.

This typical bistro looks a little intimidating from the outside: it's always packed with locals, and you can't help but get the feeling that you could be gatecrashing some private do by entering it. The buzzy, plain-looking room is famous for its mussels and its bouillabaisse; prices are reasonable, with the four-course menu great value. A quick word about service, while we're here, and that word is 'sucks': while the staff are friendly enough, some seem to forget they're working in a restaurant, and you'll wait ages for your food. That said, you'll still leave feeling mighty satisfied. This is Belgium as she is known.

Jacques

44 quai aux Briques (02 513 27 62). Métro Ste-Catherine. **Meals served** noon-2.30pm, 6.30-10.30pm Mon-Sat. **Average** €€€. **Credit** MC, V.

A real favourite among Bruxellois, Jacques oozes traditional Belgian charm; in summer, when the huge windows come down and the restaurant meets the street, it's particularly delightful. The old-fashioned wood-panelled interior and tiled floors give the place its atmosphere – although the new back room, with its cleaner-cupboard feel, doesn't quite meet the standards set out front – while diners tuck in enthusiastically to a variety of fishy dishes. Among the menu's highlights are a thick slice of turbot with mousseline sauce, and gluggy eels in green sauce. Wines can be on the pricey side, but the house white is a perfectly decent Alsace.

Le Jardin de Catherine

5-7 place Ste-Catherine (02 513 92 62). Métro Ste-Catherine. **Meals served** noon-2.30pm, 7-11pm Mon-Fri, Sun; 7-11pm Sat. **Average** €€€. **Credit** AmEx, DC, MC, V.

Lurking behind a terraced frontage is one of the most enticing gardens in the centre of the city, a garden that, one presumes, is responsible for the name of this restaurant. Great rolling sun (and rain) shades protect the crisp white linen tables, water features play enchantingly

RESTAURANT

within earshot and vast olive oil pitchers spill over with flowers and plants. Ah, but only inside the restaurant is bereft of any charm whatsoever, meaning you're best off heading here when the sun's out and sticking to the Jardin's *jardin*. Year-round, the food is perfectly balanced, French-influenced fish and seafood, the clientele well-heeled and the service immaculate.

Le Loup-Galant ★

4 quai aux Barques (02 219 99 98). Métro Ste-Catherine. **Meals served** noon-2.30pm, 7-10pm Tue-Sat. **Average** €€€€. **Credit** AmEx, DC, MC, V.
Tucked at the end of Ste-Catherine's main fishy drag, this smart little restaurant sits in a former house whose uninspiring suburban interior doesn't live up to its 17th-century origins. That said, there is plenty of space for large tables, and in summer, the brick-walled terrace proves understandably popular. The menu is rather short, but full of imaginative fish and seafood based along traditional French lines. The bouillabaisse is the star turn: it arrives in two portions, each with different varieties of fish. It's a little on the expensive side, but you're paying not just for the fine food, but for the quietly tangible and appealing exclusivity.

Le Vismet ★

23 place Ste-Catherine (02 218 85 45). Métro Ste-Catherine. **Meals served** noon-2.30pm, 7-11.30pm Tue-Sat. **Average** €€€. **Credit** AmEx, MC, V.
This relative newcomer to Ste-Catherine has provided some competition for some of its stuffier neighbours. The design is lofty minimalism: all red brick and exposed ventilation shafts, with the tables fantastically simple boards on four legs. And the food comes courtesy of chef Tom Decroos, who received his training under Yves Mattagne at the award-winning Sea Grill (*see p34*) and now toils away frantically in an open kitchen, preparing fish delivered fresh from Brittany twice weekly. The mixed grill of Atlantic fish fillets is amazingly fresh, as is the selection of seafood that includes langoustines and clams. The menu changes regularly according to season and what Decroos believes is suitable for the standard of his kitchen. It's a pity that the ever-so-slightly snooty service doesn't match the food. Forget shining the forks, chum: just bring the damn meal.

Le Vistro

16 quai aux Briques (02 512 41 81). Métro Ste-Catherine. **Meals served** noon-3pm, 6.30-10.45pm Mon-Fri; 6.30-10.45pm Sat. **Average** €€€. **Credit** AmEx, DC, MC, V.
Blink and you'll miss Le Vistro, a tiny eatery that sits unassumingly among a terrace of bigger properties. Inside, it's as cosy as you might expect, done out in raw

brick with wooden tables and chairs; in summer, there's also a canopied alfresco area across the road. The restaurant differentiates itself from its neighbours with its enormous plates of fruits de mer: vast zinc trays balance precariously on a tripod, dripping with oysters, mussels, clams, whelks, little black things for which you need a pin, crab and – if you want to pay extra – great pink lobster. If you need help passing time while this feast is prepared, wine can be served by the pot, a Lyonnaise-style bottle filled from the tap.

International

Gazebo

5 place du Nouveau Marché-aux-Grains (02 514 26 96). Métro Ste-Catherine. **Meals served** 7pm-late Mon, Tue, Thur-Sat. **Average** €€€. **Credit** MC, V.

A few years ago, New Yorker Lee Better opened a restaurant in the EU Quarter, where the food reflected the Greek origins of her hubby-chef Argirios Carananos. Now, though, the Betters have bettered themselves and opened a smart, minimalist place downtown, whose more eclectic menu better reflects the broad mix of nationalities who live in Brussels. The restaurant has a great atmosphere: it's relaxed and cosy, and Lee will make you feel as though you've known her all your life. Note the rainbow flag flying outside: it's not an exclusively gay restaurant, by any means, but Lee does like her boys and hosts occasional special evenings here for local gay professionals.

I Latini

2 place Ste-Catherine (02 502 50 30). Métro Ste-Catherine. **Meals served** noon-2.30pm, 6.30-11pm daily. **Average** €€€. **Credit** AmEx, DC, MC, V.

I Latini is a big and unashamedly blowsy restaurant: it's all done out in mock sienna wall-wash, with commedia dell'arte characters frescoed into the plaster. Such decor is not to everyone's taste, but the food hits the spot: this is basic Italian fare at its most enjoyable, served with the requisite Italian verve and the best Italian wine. It's no theme park, but it does rest very firmly on its laurels, with a good bunch of basil thrown in for good measure. Being Italiano in the middle of this fishy district does give it novelty value, but punters come here for business meals as well as big social meets. Friendly and fun, then, neither of which is in any way a bad thing.

Da Mimmo

165 rue Antoine Dansaert (02 223 23 07). Pré-métro Bourse. **Meals served** noon-3pm, 6.30-11pm Mon-Sat. **Average** €€. **Credit** AmEx, MC, V.

The shop attached to **François** (2 quai aux Briques) is a fish and seafood speciality grocer's, and stocks such goodies as ready-to-grill scallops on the shell, eels in green sauce and giant prawns in garlic. There are also lobster and oysters ready to go.

Domenico Carlucci's intimate restaurant on one of Brussels' trendiest streets is a little pizza perfection. There are 25 varieties on the menu, taking in ingredients both expected and exotic. The vegetarian range is especially fine: for once, they're not just spread sadly with cheap tomato paste but composed of vegetables from the antipasti menu, so hearty artichokes and slabs of red pepper in olive oil are the order of the day. The cool atmosphere is totally in keeping with the area, and ensures that the fashion-conscious locals are happy to call in and be part of the action. But in a part of town where image is everything, Mimmo wins for its pure, unpretentious quality and keen prices.

Strofilia

11 rue du Marché aux Porcs (02 512 32 93). Métro Ste-Catherine. **Open** 7pm-midnight Mon-Thur, Sun; 7pm-1am Fri, Sat. **Average** €€. **Credit** AmEx, MC, V.
Let's be clear from the start: this is not a plate-smashing, ouzo-swigging sort of place. No, this is Greek chic, where locals get dressed up to the nines for a night out with close friends and loved ones. Its setting in an old pig market gives it a lofty New York feel, but pass downstairs to the cellar, decked out as a late bar, and you'll be transported to medieval Spain. And it's in the shadows of this vaulted cave that the restaurant's fine Greek wines are kept behind locked grilles; all have been hand-picked by Stefanos Svanias, who had already built his Brussels reputation with the Ouzerie before heading here. The menu is big on meze, the service big on detail.

Bars

Chez Martine

37 rue de Flandre (02 512 43 23). Métro Ste-Catherine. **Open** noon-1am Tue-Fri; 4pm-1am Sat. **No credit cards**.
AKA Chez Haesendonck or Le Daringman, this wonderful venue is a real in-the-know place, hidden on a dark stretch between the Flemish fashion quarter and the canal. Chez Martine embraces the lower echelons of Flemish bohemia, set somewhere between the stars and the gutter. Entertainingly retro – old Stella signs, Ella posters, house plants *du choix* from the '50s – and swathed in smoke (you could be forgiven for thinking you were at a Rick Wakeman concert, were such a thing in any way forgivable), the bar draws a colourful collection of characters, if occasionally too many for comfort. Within a year, it could justifiably lay claim to opening up this forgotten corner of Ste-Catherine, even if locals are happy with how it is.

Kafka

6 rue de la Vierge Noire (02 513 54 89). Métro/Pré-métro De Brouckère. **Open** 4pm-2am Mon-Thur; 4pm-4am Fri, Sat; 5pm-2am Sun. **No credit cards**.

Any place that keeps late opening hours on Sunday night must have something going for it. Certainly, the Kafka is more than just a pretty clock face: it's got vodkas and genevers and then some, and a clientele of real rough diamonds, pseudo-literary politicos whose discourse dribbles into drivel by the time they've gone from pear to peach on the fruit gin front. Obscure games of cards pass the time once speech functions cease, which they inevitably will. Franz has got nothing to do with it whatsoever, of course; any such homage would be laughed out of town.

Monk

42 rue Ste-Catherine (02 503 08 80). Métro Ste-Catherine. **Open** 4pm-2am Mon-Fri, Sun; 4pm-3am Fri, Sat. **No credit cards**.

Although the immediate quay area around Ste-Catherine is crowded with little bars, few warrant further attention. Monk is unusual in that someone has taken the trouble and considerable expense to create a kind of JD Wetherspoon à la Belge out of what was obviously for many years a bog-standard local. Set in a 17th-century gabled house close to the main square, it's set apart by its big picture window and contemporary logo, a lettered square used on its sign and stickers. The interior comprises a long, dark wood bar, soft-lit by railway carriage wall lights above a panelled mirrored row. Monk is trying to attract a reasonably stylish, moneyed young crowd. Once they come – if they come – it could detract some of the spotlight away from the parallel rue Antoine Dansaert, which would be no bad thing.

La Tentation

28 rue de Laeken (02 211 40 99/www.latentation.org). Métro/Pré-métro De Brouckère. **Open** 8am-midnight Mon-Thur; 8am-2am Fri; 6pm-2am Sat. **No credit cards**.

Brussels' considerable Spanish community – mainly Asturians and Galicians destined for low-paid jobs – gather chiefly in small private members' bars dotted around the Lower Town. La Tentation, a bar, restaurant, concert venue and Galician cultural centre, has begun to reverse this solitary trend. Set in a huge industrial space sprawling over two floors, the Temptation buzzes on events nights but feels pretty lonely on quieter weekdays, when voices echo around its brick walls. The food is the usual selection of tapas, cheeses and cold meats, with authentic beers and liqueurs to match.

One of the best poultry and game shops in Brussels is **Matthys & Van Gaever** (20 rue Melsens). From wild quail to fillet of deer, it's all here and ready for the pot.

St-Géry

St-Géry

PLACE DU
NOUVEAU
MARCHE
AUX GRAINS

NIEUWE
GRAANMARKT

Ste-Catherine

PLACE STE-
CATHERINE

RUE DU REMPART DES MOINES

A DANSAERTSTRAAT

RUE DE LA BRAIE

RUE STE-CATHERINE

RUE DE LA VIERGE NOIRE

RUE DU MARCHE
AUX POULETS

RUE DES
POISONNIERS

RUE DU BOULET

R DU VIEUX MARCHE AUX GRAINS

Musée
Album

CHARTREUX

P. DEFEUX

VR VAN VAAK STRAAT

⑪

③ ⑫

⑧

①

RUE DES

⑥

RUE ORTS

PLACE DU JARDIN
AUX FLEURS

RUE ST-CHRISTOPHE

ARTEVELDE

⑬

PONT DE LA CARPE

⑰

Bourse

BLOEMENHOF-
PLEIN

⑯

⑦

PLACE
ST-GÉRY

⑮

RUE J VAN PRAET

⑤

Ⓜ Bourse

RUE H MAUS

RUE VAN

RUE DE LA GRANDE ILE

Halles
St-Géry

RUE DE

⑨

Scientastic
Museum

RUE DES SIX JETONS

ST-GORIKS-
PLEIN

②

⑭

BORGVAL

Notre Dame
aux Riches–
Claires

RUE ST-GÉRY

RUE DES PIERRES

⑩

RUE DES RICHES–CLAIRES

ZESPENNINGEN

④

BOULEVARD ANSPACH

Pré-métro ☎ 02-52-55-55-55

ST GÉRY

RUE DU

AUX CHARBON

LOMBARD

D'ANDERLECHT

Notre Dame du
Bon Secours

RUE DU MIDI

RUE DES

PLACE
FONTAINAS-
PLEIN

RUE DU MARCHE

RUE DES G CARMES

ANDERLECHTSE-STEENWEG

ZUIDSTRAAT

R DES SOIGNIES

RUE DE LA VERDURE

RUE DES
BOGARDS

LOWER TOWN

LOOFSTRAAT

Ⓜ Anneessens

RUE DES ALEXIENS

RUE DE L'ETUVE

BOULEVARD MAURICE-LEMONNIER

RUE

HELMONT

RUE DU MIDI

BODEGHEM

PLACE
ANNEESSENS
PLEIN

KAZERNESTRAAT

RUE VAN HELMONT

RUE P DE
CHAMPAGNE

PLACE
ROUPPE

0   150 m
0   150 yds

© Copyright Time Out Group 2003

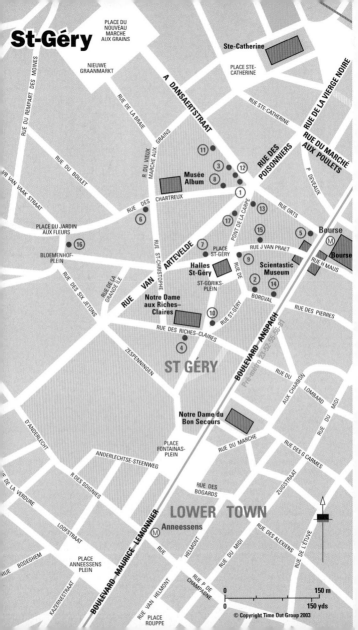

What was once a run-down area, trapped between Grand' Place and Ste-Catherine, is now a thriving and upmarket area with a mass of bars, a lively restaurant scene and a small but ever-developing Chinatown. The renovation of the symbolic centre of the area, the Halles de St-Géry (an old covered dairy market), sparked off a designer revolution led by Fred Nicolay (*see p68* **Right said Fred**). Along with the development of the trendy fashion street rue Antoine Dansaert, it's attracted young professionals of all nationalities back to the city centre, upping property prices in the process. Yet St-Géry's old charm remains and its tangle of small streets is well worth exploring.

Restaurants
Belgian & French

Le Petit Boxeur

Look out for the **Chez Jef et Fils** food stall opposite the Bourse. Here, you can buy bowls of steaming escargots (whelks); in winter, it also has a hot chestnut stand.

3 Borgval (02 511 40 00). Pré-métro Bourse.
Meals served 7pm-midnight Tue-Sun. **Average** €€€.
Credit AmEx, MC, V.

The little boxer looks like a little boxer chocolates from the outside. Through the tiny frontage, you can see a small, camp, wooden-Gothic dining room with traditional dark woods to keep it on the right side of respectable. A bar dominates the entrance, though this is more for service than punters. The food's the thing here: trendy French dishes served to trendy Belgians who come here for a little intimacy. The menu includes interesting variations on known quantities: lasagne is made not with ground beef but with finely sliced squid stuffed with tuna, while a fish terrine is served up in the sushi style, raw with a dash of caviar. Sounds good? Well, it is, but you can't help feeling you're paying a little too much for what is essentially brasserie-style food. But then this is St-Géry, and that's the way it is around here.

In 't Spinnekopke ★

1 place du Jardin aux Fleurs (02 511 86 95). Pré-métro Bourse. **Meals served** noon-3pm, 6-11pm Mon-Fri; 6-11pm Sat. **Average** €€€. **Credit** AmEx, DC, MC, V.
You can't miss this Flemish-style restaurant, a 17th-century cottage set among an eclectic range of more modern buildings on this pretty, recently furbished square. Enter through the front door – ducking your head

Breaking bread

Like all good ideas, the concept behind **Le Pain Quotidien** (16 rue Antoine Dansaert, 02 502 23 61, www.painquotidien.com, plus branches in Brussels and Antwerp) is simple. For one, the food is uncomplicated and tasty: highlighted by the titular *pain*, a naturally fermented wholewheat sour-dough variety, and supported by croissants, cakes and other lunchy, brunchy items. In addition, the decor is plain and attractive: antique country furniture, wooden dressers, thick floorboards and marble counter-tops. Sympathetic staff, too.

However, the masterstroke behind Le Pain Quotidien, the reason for its success, sits in the middle of the room. It doesn't look like much, just a vast, scrubbed pine kitchen table. But it turns Le Pain Quotidien from a café into something more, and has turned the operation, founded by renowned Belgian baker Alain Coumont, from a Brussels experiment into

a major international brand with branches all over Belgium and France, and in places as far away as Rome, Geneva, New York and Los Angeles.

The ever-reserved Brits may blanche at the idea of lunching with complete strangers, but the Belgians have taken to it like fish to the proverbial H_2O. The table gives each branch a community feel. Regulars come and go, popping by for a cuppa and croissant or something more substantial; a roast beef and caper mayonnaise sandwich, say. Some natter the morning away, while others read in silence. Whatever: it's up to you. It's meant to be relaxed and relaxing, so relax.

Le Pain Quotidien's takeaway bakeries are not to be sniffed at either; serving breads, pastries, fruit tarts and the practically legendary bombe au chocolat, a rich chocolate-mousse cake, they're extremely popular with locals. And the food served in the café is just fine, too. But really, it's the table that makes the place. Pull up a chair.

Au Suisse (73-75 boulevard Anspach) is nothing much to do with Switzerland but all to do with Belgium. There's a deli on one side and a lunch spot on the other; sit in 1950s splendour and tuck into fresh baguettes and home-made ice-cream.

In 't Spinnekopke. *See p60.*

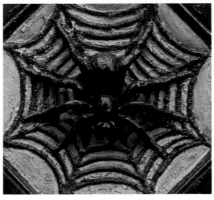

Thiên. *See p66.*

as you do so – and you'll find yourself in a different world, one of rabbits cooked in beer, beef cooked in beer and customers cooked in beer. It's a seriously heavy menu, but it comes with the seal of true Bruxelloise authenticity. The new square has brought a new terrace for the restaurant, a delightfully olde worlde setting surrounded by trailing geraniums.

International

Bonsoir Clara ★

22-26 rue Antoine Dansaert (02 502 09 90). Pré-métro Bourse. **Meals served** noon-2.30pm, 7-10.30pm Mon-Thur; noon-2.30pm, 7pm-midnight Fri; 7pm-midnight Sat; 7-10.30pm Sun. **Average** €€€. **Credit** AmEx, MC, V.

Bonsoir Clara has long been pinned as the restaurant that first dragged the St-Géry area upscale, simultaneously starting things off for entrepreneur Fred Nicolay. Now the restaurant sits there as if it owns the *quartier*. A glimpse through the windows, which open on to the street in summer, reveal zinc tables with an understated single bloom, red brick walls and primary-colour light squares giving a feel of postmodernist comfort. The menu is French-influenced with trendy Tuscan overtones: seared this with a coulis of that, piled high on the plate and dotted with olive oil, with a better-than-average choice for vegetarians. If you want to look like a regular, place your mobile neatly next to the cutlery.

Divino

56 rue des Chartreux (02 503 39 09). Pré-métro Bourse. **Meals served** noon-2.30pm, 6.30-11.30pm Mon-Fri; 6.30-11.30pm Sat, Sun. **Average** €€. **Credit** AmEx, MC, V.

Muscling in on the feelgood factor that's swept St-Géry of late, Divino is a relative newcomer to the area. Owner Moses Guez seemed to import a whole set of diners through the freshly painted doors when it opened, a youngish, well-heeled set wearing square-rimmed glasses with their business suits. What's surprising is that the restaurant has remained busy after the initial excitement left, though the modern Italian cooking and homely local feel both appeal. The scrubbed tables, set in a retro minimalist style, provide a home for pizzas (parma ham and goat's cheese, say) and other more innovative dishes (a version of carpaccio of beef with rocket).

Indus Valley

37 place St-Géry (02 512 63 89). Pré-métro Bourse. **Meals served** noon-3pm, 7-11pm Tue-Sun. **Average** €€€. **Credit** AmEx, DC, MC, V.

Slap bang on the square, between the Zebra and the Roi des Belges bars, is the bottle-green Indus Valley. The location's prime: publicans would kill for it. But Indus

Place St-Géry is heaving in the summer, with large café terraces on each corner. Find a table wherever you can: it's all much of a muchness.

St-Géry

Valley has it, and sits there coolly drawing in drinkers who, after a few blanche beers, realise they're actually a little hungry. The interior is nothing special: the tables are screened from the street by straggly house plants, and the lighting is on the bright side of brash. But there's nothing wrong with the food, drawn from a standard menu. Indus Valley advertises its specialities as Pakistani and Indian food, though it's no great leap from the sort of sub-continental food found in innumerable British restaurants.

Da Kao

38 rue Antoine Dansaert (02 512 67 16). Pré-métro Bourse. **Meals served** noon-3pm, 6pm-midnight daily. **Average** €. **No credit cards**.

Chinese whispers

As you cross the road from the Bourse and walk into the narrow rue Jules van Praet, you'll be faced with a barrage of neon, bamboo and stone Buddhas. You have stepped into Chinatown. However, unlike in many other cities, Brussels' Chinatown is no great tourist attraction – no pagoda phone boxes here, no sir – but a rather loose community that's home to several worthwhile restaurants.

Rue Jules van Praet is a colourful strip of restaurants whose cuisine covers much of South-east Asia, bearing alluring names like **Bambou Fleur** (No.13) and **Rêves d'Asie** (No.19). Most hedge their bets and serve up combinations of regional food such as Thai-Viet or Chinese-Viet, with only a few sticking to their guns and homing in on one country. Those that do include **Davi** (No.20) or **Phat Thai** (No.32), which serve typical and perfectly acceptable Thai food of the lemongrass

and coconut milk variety. The only truly Chinese restaurant here is **China Town** (No.1), up a steep flight and above the Fortis Bank.

Round the corner and into pont de la Carpe is a tiny Thai restaurant, **Bois Luang** (No.3), that serves fantastically pungent Thai dishes with fantastically slow service. Opposite it is Vietnamese snack-resto **Hong Hua** (No.10), which, along with **Da Kao** (*see p64*) and **Thiên** (*see p66*), offers Chinatown's best food at its best prices.

The Chinatown theme runs into Ste-Catherine. Here, oriental supermarkets take pride of place, among them the massive but unhelpful **Kam Yuen** (1 rue Ste-Catherine) and the slightly cheerier but over-stuffed **Thai Supermarket** (3 rue Ste-Catherine). New shops seem to be popping up all the time around here, and are beginning to give the area some much-needed identity.

Archiduc. *See p66.*

Da Kao is one of many caff-style oriental eateries in the area, but it seems to beat all its rivals on price. The biggest mistake here is to over-order because of the assumption that cheap equals meagre. As an order of any noodle dish will illustrate, nothing could be further from the truth. Da Kao is totally without pretension, and pretty much without frills: you'll be seated, you'll be served, you'll be given the bill, all the while with crowds coming and going around you. Accept it for what it is and you won't be disappointed. Whatever happens, you certainly won't leave hungry.

Kasbah

20 rue Antoine Dansaert (02 502 40 26). Pré-métro Bourse. **Meals served** noon-2pm, 7-11pm daily.
Average €€. **Credit** AmEx, MC, V.
A window filled with oranges leads you into a bazaar of Moroccan lamps and oil burners at this magical spot. The richly authentic atmosphere is reflected in the food, a goodly selection of meze, couscous and spiced grills; it's a perfect place for mixed company, veggie or not. That

said, it does gets packed, especially at weekends when groups meet up for a pre-hitting-the-town supper. Book ahead if possible.

Shamrock

27 rue Jules van Praet (02 511 49 89). Pré-métro Bourse.
Meals served 7pm-midnight Tue-Sun. **Average** €.
No credit cards.

The Indian subcontinent blends surprisingly well with Belgian bizarre in this tacky, slightly dingy but ultimately irresistible curry house. The name? Well, this was an Irish pub in a previous life, and the Indian eatery has simply cuckooed in on what was left of the boozer. What was formerly the bar is now a service area, offering ample room in which the head of family prepares the bills and smokes to his heart's content. His sons and daughters cook and serve the food – each dish comes in three chilli strengths – while their children play until bedtime. The food's cheap, but portions are on the small side; if in doubt, over-order.

Thiên ★

12 rue Van Artevelde (02 511 34 80). Metro/Pré-métro Brouckère. **Meals served** noon-3pm, 6-11pm Mon, Tue, Thur-Sun. **Average** €. **Credit** AmEx, MC, V.

What a wonder this little Vietnamese snack-resto is. A friendly young family runs it, offering great steaming bowls of soup, lacquered duck, plump prawns and crisp stir-fries to an appreciative crowd. The decor is kitsch, the food is top-quality and the kitchen is inhabited by the smallest chef you have ever seen, her white hat bobbing above the counter-top as she shakes the wok and feeds the entire restaurant. She, too, is a wonder, and helps to make Thiên one of the best places to eat in town.

Le Greenwich.
See p70.

Bars

Archiduc

6 rue Antoine Dansaert (02 512 06 52). Pré-métro Bourse.
Open 4pm-dawn daily. **Credit** AmEx, DC, MC, V.

The duke of all dives, the baron of all bars, the art deco Archiduc was the prime mover in the rapid development of this now-fashionable enclave. Opened at the same time and on the same street as the first designer clothes stores of Flemish provenance, it soon proved the perfect vehicle for fashionistas and their chic cohorts; that vehicle proved to be an ocean liner, its two-floor interior resembling the smooth curves of a ballroom drifting across the Atlantic. The ambience is flung further forwards by the tinklings of a jazz pianist and the skill of a staff adept at waltzing

through the mingle with trays of cocktail glasses rattling at shoulder level. Doorbell entry, pre-dawn drinking and demi-monde regulars dot the 'i' of the illusion.

Bar à Tapas

11 rue Borgval (02 502 66 02). Pré-métro Bourse.
Open noon-1am Mon-Fri; 6pm-late Sat, Sun.
Credit MC, V.

Rare is the tapas bar worth recommending, but this one in the heart of St-Géry stands out thanks to its role as a major gathering point. As they do in Spain, folks snack, chat and enjoy a couple of aperitifs before moving on elsewhere, and with no mock Mexicana or microwaved merluza in sight. Set on a busy corner, the chalked-up lunch specials dragging in an ever-changing mix of tourists and office workers, the Bar à Tapas changes

Pick up a bento, a packed sushi lunchbox, at **Sushi Factory** (28 place St-Géry).

Right said Fred

Before Frédéric Nicolay claimed it, St-Géry was a grey place. 'The area had been left to rot,' recalls the entrepreneur. 'Right in the centre of Brussels, too. It seemed ripe for opportunity.' Nicolay seized it, and now presides over a 15-strong empire of bars in town.

A trained cook, Nicolay had previously worked with Alain Coumont – before he launched the **Pain Quotidien** chain, for which *see p60* **Breaking bread** – and ran a couple of restaurants 'on a sixpence' before deciding to swap the frying pan for the cocktail shaker in St-Géry. The fashion quarter of rue Antoine Dansaert was about to burgeon on its doorstep. Nicolay's timing couldn't have been better.

He started with the **Mappa Mundo** (2-6 rue du Pont de la Carpe, 02 514 35 55), then opened the **Zebra** (33 place St-Géry, 02 511 09 01) and **Le Roi des Belges** (35 rue Jules van Praet, 02 503 43 00). All were brash, high-concept style bars, each themed up to a point, but all very much of a type. They worked. 'The whole town followed us, place to place, reviving urban space,' says Nicolay. 'We boomed.'

Some travel writers, bored with having to describe the Falstaff year after year, began to equate St-Géry with cutting edge – erroneously. In fact, out-of-season visitors may be disappointed. Surrounding the box-shaped old covered market on place St-Géry are resto-bars so standardised their very emptiness conjures images of that apes-meet-box scene from *2001: A Space Odyssey*. On summer evenings, however, when the job-lot terrace tables fill with lively banter, St-Géry can be a lot of fun. But cutting-edge? Perhaps not.

Nicolay's brand established, he's run with it to lucrative effect. Expansion has involved a modern European restaurant of considerable repute, **Bonsoir Clara** (*see p63*), and a move into the university quarter at Ixelles' far southern end with **Le Tavernier** (445 chaussée de Boondael, 02 640 71 91). A visit to this Hoxton-style hip resto-bar reveals the backers behind the Nicolay empire; over the building, in lurid red, shines a huge sign whose logo will be familiar to beer-lovers the world over. 'Of all my exploits,' says Nicolay, 'the most successful has been to gather a hard-working team around me, and especially to have convinced the Duvel Moortgat brewery to venture their money on the strength of my ideas.'

Nicolay's most recent idea has been to revive the far stretch of rue Antoine Dansaert by the canal, a desolate area previously only alleviated by squat-style galleries. The wantonly red (coincidence?) **Walvis** bar (rue Antoine Dansaert 209, 02 219 95 32) is the pioneering venture. And then? 'We're looking at a new place... In London!' World domination beckons.

Put your feet up and have a decent cup of tea in **AM Sweet** (4 rue des Chartreux). Take some spiced fruit cake or buy some dainty hand-made chocolates to take home.

mood of an evening when the lights flicker in the twisted lampshades and the intimate interior fills with expectant punters. A huge selection of tapas too; altogether, perfect for a bunch of weekenders on a communal jolly.

Le Coaster

28 rue des Riches Claires (no phone). Pré-métro Bourse.
Open 8pm-late Mon-Sat. **No credit cards**.
This is a St-Géry hardy perennial, mainly because it offers attractive advantages for the fun-seeking young regulars without the prices and pretensions of the bulk of the bars nearby. These advantages may be listed in interchangeable order as (a) table football, (b) liberal happy hours up to 11pm, (c) danceable music without the rigmarole of nightclub palaver, and (d) laughably easy skirt/shirt. In this way, the two rooms of this small red-brick building get packed to their 17th-century beams, and weekend nights can only really be enjoyed with a loud group of people. But of a post-midnight Wednesday, post St-Géry barhop, the Coaster and its spinning figures come into their own.

Le Coq

14 rue Auguste Orts (02 514 24 14). Pré-métro Bourse.
Open 10am-4am Mon-Sat. **No credit cards**.
A proper bar. No branded bar staff, no artsy name, no gimmicky fittings. The Cock: come and get it, pure and simple. Beer, neon, red banquettes and a big-bellied barman equally interested in shooting pinball as serving young punters Stellas, which he calls over as 'cadets' to the wrinkly beer pouress behind the modest counter. But for a constant downpour of weepy French pop, you could hear the tabby cat snoring on the beertray she claimed as hers one particular pinball session. Bar snacks run to cheese and ham toasties complemented by the dismissive plonk of a ketchup bottle. Laudably unpretentious and justifiably popular.

Gecko

16 place St-Géry (no phone). Pré-métro Bourse.
Open noon-1am Mon-Wed, Sun; 4pm-1am Thur-Sat.
No credit cards.
A strange, intimate bar that's yet to find its core clientele since opening in September 2002. Encrusted with dozens of tiny, shiny bright surfaces, the chameleon-like Gecko seems to offer beads and mirrors to the natives without showing any true colours, though its modest daily menu is a cut above the rest and its cocktails are a fine mix of old favourites. Thursdays are given over to readings and acoustic evenings; a half-decent DJ might shake things up a bit. If successful, it could pull discerning clientele away from the branded bars around the square opposite. If not, it could be broken up for earrings.

Le Greenwich

7 rue des Chartreux (02 511 41 67). Pré-métro Bourse.
Open 11am-1am Mon-Thur, Sun; 11am-2am Fri, Sat.
No credit cards.
Past the slow creak of the wooden door, the other side of
the ornate partition separating window seats from sedate
interior, a library hush signals a sense of decorum to be
assumed upon entering. Clack! A chess piece moves.
Tock! An oval clock ticks over the elaborate bar counter.
Tack! Another tupperware box of chess pieces is taken
from the middle pillar and placed on one of four rows of
marble tables as a board is unfolded. Amid the
concentrated rolling of tobacco, an eyebrow is raised, then
straightened once more. Magritte hustled pictures and
Bobby Fischer hustled chess here, but please don't shout
about it. Don't shout about anything, in fact. Order up a
drink, open up a book and observe.

Le Java

31 rue St-Géry (02 512 37 16). Pré-métro Bourse.
Open 5pm-2am daily. **No credit cards.**
An imposingly cool bar composing the bow of St-Géry as
it meets rue de la Grande Ile, Le Java makes the best of
its three-sided space. Flemish in origin, international in
clientele, it's great when all you want is a quiet drink amid
attractive decor and among attractive company. The
interior is dominated by a heavy round bar counter,
footrailed by twisted metal and offset by half a tree and
half a globe. Less obtuse attention would reveal it veering
into the truly naff: the framed 'Ask the Menu' sign
advertising the daily specials, for example. Bel pils and
Steendonk on draught, and the welcome smile that greets
ordering a glass of same, more than make up for it.

MP3 Café

17-19 rue du Pont de la Carpe (info@mp3discobar.com).
Pré-métro Bourse. **Open** hours vary. **No credit cards.**
A new bar on the block around a square already totally
swamped with them, the MP3 Café is attention-
warranting as one of Brussels' few DJ bars. And it's not
a bad place, either. Spotlights over a curving bar counter
highlight a row of brown stools and a bar length of
posable mirror. Facing this across a narrow space is a
stretch of banquette leading to a modest raised dance
area, two semi-circles of seats and a disco ball. All of
this is mere decoration – a hindrance, even – to the buzz
of activity by the decks at the far end of the bar counter,
and the confined vibrant dancing post-midnight. The
DJs could do with a little polishing, but that's Brussels
for you – hey, there might just be some work in this town
for you. A nearby larger version of same might empty
the place, but not just yet.

Den Teepot
(66 rue des
Chartreux) is
an absolutely
PC organic
and
vegetarian
grocer's
selling
everything
from milk to
Japanese
seaweed, plus
grain bread
and pastries.

Sablon & Upper Town

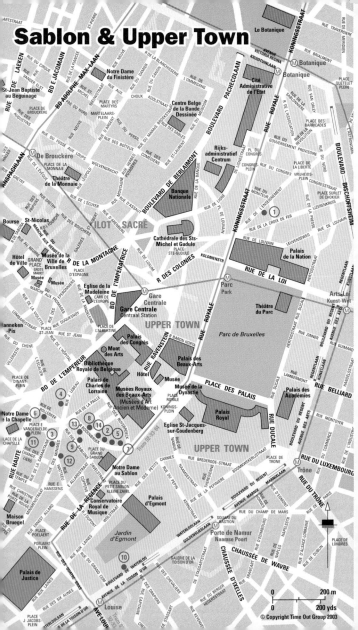

Sablon & Upper Town

ARTSTRAAT
RUE DE TRAVERSIERE
MERIDIEN
Le Botanique
KONINGSSTRAAT
RUE BRIALMONT
AVENUE VICTORIA REGINA
KRUIDTUINLAAN
Botanique
PLACE QUETELET PLEIN

LAEKEN
RUE DU CIRQUE
ST-PIERRE
R DE LA FIANCEE
RUE DE LA BLANCHISSERIE
RUE DE L'OMMEGANG
BOULEVARD PACHECOLAAN
Botanique
Cité Administrative de l'Etat
RUE ROYALE
RUE DE LA SABLONNIERE
RUE VAN ORLEY
RUE DE L'ASSOCIATION
PLACE DES BARRICADES

BD ADOLPHE MAX LAAN
Notre Dame du Finistère
RUE AUX CHOUX
KOOLSTRAAT
Centre Belge de la Bande Dessinée
PLACE DE LA REVOLUTION
VRIJHEIDS-PLEIN
BOULEVARD BISCHOFFSHEIM
CONGRESSTRAAT

St-Jean Baptiste au Beguinage
PLACE DE BROUCKERE
RUE DES AUGUSTINS
RUE DU FOSSE AUX LOUPS
Rijks-administratief Centrum
RUE DE LIGNE
PL DU CONGRES
RUE DU CONGRES
CONGRES-PLEIN
PLACE SURLET DE CHOKIER
RUE DE LA LIBERTE
BOULEVARD DU NORD

De Brouckère
PLACE DE LA MONNAIE
Théâtre de la Monnaie
WOLVENGRACHT
BOULEVARD DE BERLAIMONT
Banque Nationale
RUE DU MONITEUR
RUE DE L'ENSEIGNEMENT
KONINGSSTRAAT

Bourse
St-Nicolas
ILOT SACRÉ
Cathédrale des Sts-Michel et Gudule
RUE DE LA CROIX DE FER
Palais de la Nation

Hôtel de Ville
Musée de la Ville de Bruxelles
DE LA MONTAGNE
KOLONIENSTR
RUE DE LOUVAIN
LEUVENSEWEG
RUE DE LA LOI

Musée
Eglise de la Madeleine
Gare Centrale
Centraal Station
UPPER TOWN
RUE ROYALE
Parc Park
Théâtre du Parc
Arts-Loi Kunst-Wet

Manneken-Pis
PLACE DE L'ALBERTINE
Palais des Congrès
Mont des Arts
Parc de Bruxelles
RUE DUCALE

Bibliothèque Royale de Belgique
Palais de Charles de Lorraine
Hôtel
Musée
Palais des Beaux-Arts
PLACE DES PALAIS

Notre Dame la Chapelle
Musées Royaux des Beaux-Arts (Musées d'Art Ancien et Moderne)
Musée de la Dynastie
Palais Royal
Palais des Académies
RUE BELLIARD

PLACE DE LA CHAPELLE
Eglise St-Jacques-sur-Coudenberg
UPPER TOWN
RUE DUCALE
RUE DU LUXEMBOURG

RUE HAUTE
Notre Dame au Sablon
Conservatoire Royal de Musique
Palais d'Egmont
Trône
CHAUSSEE DE WAVRE

Maison Bruegel
Jardin d'Egmont
Porte de Namur
Naamse Poort
PLACE DE LONDRES

Palais de Justice
BOULEVARD DE WATERLOO
GALERIE DE LA TOISON D'OR

Louise
AVENUE LOUISE
CHAUSSEE D'IXELLES

0   200 m
0   200 yds

© Copyright Time Out Group 2003

Sablon, within walking distance of Grand' Place to the south-west, is Brussels' most upmarket area. The large square – tree-lined, but used chiefly as a car park – is surrounded by cafés and restaurants that attract the rich, the trendy and the body-beautiful. It's also the *quartier* for antiques and art, with expensive shops and galleries punctuating the terraces of bars and restaurants. A Sablon address is practically a status symbol in Brussels, and you can expect the local crowd to reflect such moneyed cachet. However, it's still relaxed and approachable and a mix of folk flock here, mainly in summer for the late-night buzz around the square.

Restaurants

Belgian & French

Le Cap Sablon

75 rue Lebeau (02 512 01 70). Bus 34, 95, 96. **Meals served** noon-midnight daily. **Average** €€. **Credit** MC, V.
Sablon boasts a bewildering choice of bars and restaurants, many popular even outside the predictably busy summer months. Amid this throng, though, Le Cap is one of the better bistro-type places, and one of the better-value restaurants in an area that generally attracts the rich and pretentious. Its simple, candlelit, art deco interior is home to an exciting little menu that stretches from homely staples (lamb roasted with rosemary) to sexier modern dishes (salmon in lime and honey). Although the majority of its clientele are from the wealthy, sunglasses-in-all-weather set, they're easily ignored. Settle down and make yourself at home.

Sablon & Upper Town

La Clef des Champs ★

23 rue du Rollebeek (02 512 11 93). Bus 24, 27, 95.
Meals served noon-2pm, 7.30-10pm Tue-Sat; noon-2pm
Sun. **Average** €€€. **Credit** AmEx, DC, MC, V.
It's a lovely little street, rue du Rollebeek, narrow,
cobbled, charming and full of esoteric antique shops. But
try not to pass down it without stopping in at this
enchanting restaurant. The blue and yellow decor is set
off by watercolours, photographs and even poetry by the
husband-and-wife owners, who met when she was a
dentist and he went to have a tooth pulled (and they say
love is blind). It's a friendly, cosy place, with a menu of
regional French cooking that includes preserved duck,
gratins and fish cooked in olive oil and herbs. Service is
slick and informal, the bill a pleasant surprise.

Lola ★

33 place du Grand Sablon (02 514 24 60). Bus 95,
96. **Meals served** noon-3pm, 6.30-11.30pm Mon-Fri;
noon-midnight Sat; noon-11.30pm Sun. **Average** €€€€.
Credit AmEx, MC, V.
This long, narrow restaurant has a clean, modern-retro
design, and a menu that offers classic French cooking
with a twist. Main courses include duck with mango, and
rabbit with almonds and orange blossom, plus vegetarian
dishes including risotto with garlic, mushrooms,
parmesan and basil. The diners here are a magnificent
mix of wannabes and already-ares who come to feel part
of the Sablon peer-group. Making the most of the loose-
walleted nature of its crowd, the restaurant isn't cheap,
but you're paying for the buzz. Book ahead.

Lola. *See p74.*

Maison du Boeuf ★

Hotel Hilton, 38 boulevard de Waterloo (02 504 13 34).
Métro Louise. **Meals served** noon-2.30pm, 7-10.30pm
daily. **Average** €€€€€. **Credit** AmEx, DC, MC, V.
Maison du Boeuf, one of Brussels' top restaurants, sits in
the bland tower-block Hilton near to avenue Louise. Yet
it's not just hotel guests or expense accounters who dine
here: locals, well aware of the Michelin star won by
longtime resident chef Michel Theurel, use it for their own
special treats and celebrations. Of course, there's more to
the restaurant than red meat: it specialises in fine French
fare. But its signature dish is an American rib of beef
roasted in salt crust, a meal for which diners seem
prepared to travel from afar. Decor is subtle, unobtrusive
and discreet, as one would expect in a five-star hotel's
signature restaurant. Dress smart if you don't want to
feel out of place.

Aux Marches de la Chapelle

5 place de la Chapelle (02 512 68 91). Bus 27, 48, 95, 96.
Meals served noon-2pm, 6.30-10pm Mon-Fri; 6.30-10pm
Sat. **Average** €€. **Credit** AmEx, DC, MC, V.
This belle époque brasserie is blessed with a perfect
location, opposite the stunning, renovated Eglise de la
Chapelle near place du Grand Sablon, and at the end of
the antique shop-packed rue Blaes. It makes the most of
it inside, too, with fixtures that include a splendid wooden
bar and a massive fireplace, open and wood-burning in
the winter. The menu is Belgian-based but includes other
specialities such as sauerkraut. Portions here are huge
and extremely filling, so unless you've not eaten for 48

**Claire
Fontaine**, a
tiny deli off
place du
Grand Sablon
(3 rue Ernest
Allard), is full
of goodies
from across
Europe –
including
unusual items
such as green
tomato
conserve –
as well as
prepared
takeaway
food.

Chocs away

Think Belgium, think chocolate; think chocolate, think Belgium. The phrase 'Belgian chocolate' is a global brand all of its own. Almost unquestioningly, foreigners have bought into its values: a rich taste, beautifully presented, top all-round craftsmanship, the best there is. But it's not just a luxury export item. Quite the contrary: in 1999, the Belgians bit into 82,480 tonnes of the stuff, a staggering 16.77 kilos per person. You'll need to buy some while you're here, either for yourself or for gift-hungry friends and family back home. And in Belgium, chocolate is more than just a cottage industry; there are around 500 domestic producers of handmade and factory-made items. So where to shop?

At the bottom end of the chocolate market is the ubiquitous **Léonidas** chain, where you can buy decent mixed boxes for reasonable prices at their street-frontage counters (cash only unless you spend a large sum). Mid-range chocolatiers include **Guylian** and **Corné**, both of which have fewer stores than Léonidas but are instead stocked in a number of supermarkets. The top-range chain is **Neuhaus**, whose shops generally have spectacular window displays – check the one in the covered Galeries St-Hubert – and snobby staff in white gloves.

For the best stuff, though, go to the individual shops. In **Wittamer** (6 & 12 place du Grand Sablon), **Pierre Marcolini** (39 place du Grand Sablon) and **Mary's** (73 rue Royale), you'll find exquisite collections of pralines, though none is remotely cheap. The former is perhaps the most impressive of them all, if only for its artful counter displays.

The funkiest chocolatier in town is **Planète Chocolat** (24 rue du Lombard), a fantastic shop where the brown stuff comes in all manner of shapes and forms (kissable lips, say, or a bouquet of flowers). And if you want to drop the bombe, a large cocoa-dusted chocolate mousse cake, head to **Le Pain Quotidien** (16 rue Antoine Dansaert, and branches around town). Realising that a whole cake is often too much for even the most serious chocoholic, these days it sells bombe in slices.

The general standard of chocolate excellence extends to restaurants. On a basic level, you can be sure that your chocolate mousse or gâteau dessert in restaurants will be sublime. But chocolate is also offered with coffee here, and even used in cooking main courses: it's not uncommon to find it used to flavour rich game sauces.

In truth, you're never too far from chocolate here. Nice, certainly, but there is a problem with its ubiquity. Once you've succumbed to Belgian chocolate, no other variety will ever do again. So stock up while you can.

hours or thereabouts, it pays to go easy on the starters. Lunchtimes get particularly busy with a mix of shoppers and local workers.

Tour d'y Voir

6 place du Grand Sablon (02 511 40 43). Tram 92, 93, 94/bus 34, 38. **Meals served** noon-1.45pm, 7-10.45pm Tue-Thur; noon-1.45pm, 7-11.45pm Fri, Sat. **Average** €€€€. **Credit** AmEx, DC, MC, V.
Discreetly located in an old red-brick 14th century chapel, directly above an art gallery, Tour d'y Voir is a warm, enticing place. The cuisine takes France as its base and adds lovely Belgian flourishes – Bresse chicken breast stuffed with Belgian goat's cheese and a sauce of Hoegaarden is a typical dish – and the occasional nod to elsewhere in Europe (a little couscous here, a slice of Spanish ham there). But the neatest part of the menu is the Surprise and Prestige, where you choose the basis of a course (salmon, say) and the chef does a *Ready, Steady, Cook* with it, improvising according to your tastes. If you can't be doing with all the questions, go for one of the regular set menus (€25-€55).

Au Vieux Saint Martin

38 place du Grand Sablon (02 512 64 76). Bus 95, 96. **Open** 10am-midnight daily. **Average** €€. **Credit** MC, V.
Located right in the middle of the car park known as place du Grand Sablon, Au Vieux Saint Martin is always humming, and frequently stretched to find a table for everyone. It doesn't accept reservations, so it's a case of picking your moment or preparing to wait in line. That said, there is at least a rack of glossy magazines for you to read while you wait, and it's nice to find a restaurant that extends an equal welcome to visitors after a cup of coffee or a full meal. The short menu is Brussels-based, taking in the likes of stoemp, mussels and steaks, and the portions are generous; there's also a very good wine list, with plenty of varieties available by the glass. The red walls are hung with large, contemporary paintings, and picture windows overlook the square. A good choice if you can get in.

Fish & seafood

L'Ecailler du Palais Royal ★

18 rue Bodenbroek (02 512 87 51). Bus 95, 96. **Meals served** noon-2pm, 7-10.30pm Mon-Sat. **Average** €€€€. **Credit** AmEx, DC, MC, V.
Locals regard this rather posh restaurant as one of the finest spots for seafood in the city. There's no meat on the menu: specialities include Colchester oysters, lobsters

If you need to add to your collection of dinner plates and serving bowls, buy them by the kilo at **La Vaisselle au Kilo** (8a rue Bodenbroek).

Something fishy

Life is not good for sturgeon these days. Its numbers are dwindling in Russia and Iran because of pollution, over-fishing and poaching (the robbing variety, not the cooking). Indeed, the ugly, oft-vicious creatures may have been around for 250 million years, but they're now on the doorstep of extinction.

Not only is this state of affairs bad for the natural world, it's bad for the gourmets of this world who like to snack on their eggs. For as sturgeon vanish from the world's waters, so the very future of caviar becomes doubtful. In an attempt to overcome this problem, some farmers are developing new methods to breed the fish. And at the forefront of this considerable progress is Belgium.

In order to keep the local culinary hedonists happy, farmers at the **Aqua Bio** (26

Oude Kaai, Turnhout) took the step of using huso huso, a vast breed of sturgeon.

The first cru was released at the end of 2002, and it's really not bad at all. The eggs come in two varieties, Classic and Gold, and have a wonderful texture and colour ranging from deep sea green to inky black. The taste is less salty than is usual for caviar, mainly because the eggs are fresher and the after-added salt hasn't permeated through.

Further types of caviar will follow soon from Aqua Bio. And about time, too. Creating caviar is a lengthy process: a sturgeon needs nine years' worth of comfort and happiness before it produces the correct quality of egg. But patience has at last paid off, and tins of the fish-eggs can now be found in the bigger branches of the Delhaize supermarket chain.

and steaks of turbot and tuna. The sauces are French-based and often encouragingly simple; the classic beurre-blanc is a highlight. From the outside, L'Ecailler du Palais Royal looks almost Dickensian; inside, it's traditional and formal, although many staff and diners have known each other for years. Otherwise, the atmosphere's somewhat stuffy, but if you can live with the gentlemen's club feel – and, chaps, do remember to wear a jacket and tie – then the food will make you glad you came.

International

Aux Bons Enfants
49 place du Grand Sablon (02 512 40 95). Bus 95, 96.
Meals served noon-2.30pm, 6.30-10.30pm Mon, Tue, Thur-Sun. **Average** €€. **No credit cards**.

It's good to know that in this largely expensive and exclusive area, there is a little oasis of normality in the form of a no-nonsense Italian restaurant right on place du Grand Sablon. Totally out of keeping with the classy urban joints scattered around the rest of the square, the pizzeria dares to be rustic with wooden beams and heavy kitchen-type tables. It's much like any decent honest Italian restaurant anywhere – pizzas, pastas and steaks are the order of the day and night – but this one opens on Sundays (not every restaurant round here does), won't set you back an arm and a leg, and is both cosy and comfortable. Perfect for when you've had your fill of mussels and chips and need some nursery food. It'll keep the kids happy, too.

Canne à Sucre

12 rue des Pigeons (02 513 03 72). Tram 92, 93, 94/ bus 95, 96. **Meals served** 7.30-10.30pm Tue-Sat. **Average** €€€. **Credit** MC, V.
This Caribbean place, specialising in Antillean and Creole food, is fun, fun, fun. It's also a magnificently contradictory place: bright and brash in an otherwise rather snooty area. Being from an island-based culture, the origins of the food are from the sea; Canne à Sucre makes full use of local seafood, but also imports more exotic creatures such as sea conch and land crab. Meat dishes are pork- and chicken-based. The spicy, sexy sauces include feroce, a potent blend of cod, avocado and chilli peppers. To help wash all this down, there's a vast range of fruity but deadly rum-based cocktails. Live music at the weekends makes it a bit of a party palace, and the crowds here are not slow in getting up and shaking their hips.

Les Nocturnes de Sablon takes place just before Christmas. Cafés and restaurants set up food stalls and bars on the street under white lights strung through the trees. There's live music, too, from rock to baroque.

Castello Banfi

12 rue Bodenbroek (02 512 87 94). Bus 95, 96. **Meals served** noon-2pm, 7-10pm Tue-Sat. **Average** €€€€. **Credit** AmEx, DC, MC, V.
An Italian restaurant that preens itself along with its neighbours. This is no pizza joint: Castello Banfi's kitchen cooks up smart Italian dishes, heavily influenced by France, while it doesn't even look traditionally Italian, its soft stone colours giving it a modern if '60s-influenced look. The menu's meaty, with milk-fed veal, Bleu-Belges beef, and smoked and cured hams from the Italian regions among the options. Castello Banfi imports many of its ingredients: the mascarpone, for example, is totally different – and superior – to the stuff sold in supermarkets, while the olive oil is the best first-pressed variety available. As befits the area, diners tend to be smartly turned out, so leave the jeans in the suitcase and get out that jacket and tie.

Bars

Le Bier Circus

89 rue de l'Enseignement (02 218 00 34). Métro Madou or Park. **Open** noon-2.30pm, 6pm-midnight Mon-Fri. **No credit cards**.

It's not the brightest pebble on the beach, but there are worse places to immerse yourself in local culture than the Bier Circus (around the corner from the Royal Circus, hence the name). Cartoon characters gaze down on a mixed clientele getting to grips with a list of options as long as their arm; surely, there's more gueuze here than any one man could guzzle. Once decided on the *bière du choix* – and there are plenty of Trappist varieties, too – the lucky imbiber can enjoy his trove in the company of connoisseurs and plain, simple hopheads; soon, beery friendships are struck, tardily abandoned after the strike of midnight.

Le Grain de Sable

15 place du Grand Sablon (02 514 05 83). Tram 92, 93, 94. **Open** 8am-late daily. **Credit** MC, V.

Despite its phone-box sized ground-floor bar, Le Grain de Sable is a prominent feature of Sablon bar life, partly by default – the neighbouring competition comprises the kind of bland terrace bars found on glitzy main squares from Lvov to Lisbon – and partly because of the open-jawed hours it keeps. Breakfast, lunch, liveners and late-night drinkipoos can all be taken here, but Le Grain takes it all in its stride, any hint of disturbance deflecting casually off its sand-coloured walls. In warm weather, the pavement terrace snaking around the corner becomes a right-angle of bright buzz and respectable reunion. Candlelight and Latin jazz provide additional ambience inside.

Le Perroquet

31 rue Watteeu (02 512 99 22). Tram 92, 93, 94. **Open** 10.30am-midnight Mon, Tue, Sun; 10.30am-1am Wed-Sat. **No credit cards**.

A popular haunt of well-to-do young things in summer before it's reclaimed by the autumnal flock of *stagiaires*, this authentic art nouveau corner bar is a stylish complement to the bland upmarket terrace life of place du Grand Sablon a two-minute walk away. It's quite dinky inside, so expect a scramble for a table after office hours of a Friday. But once you've settled in, a mighty range of beers and more modest selections of salads and sandwiches can be ordered – eventually – from the wait staff. All the same, the stunning stained-glass, mirrors and floor tiles make it a pleasant wait.

At **Pierre Marcolini**'s chocolate shop (39 place du Grand Sablon), there's a fountain of melted chocolate: help yourself to a spoonful or two…

EU Quarter

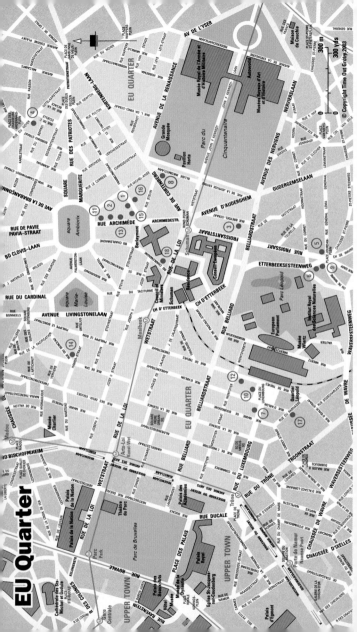

EU Quarter

The European Quarter falls into three main areas for eating and drinking. Close to the famed Berlaymont building is rue Archimède and rue Franklin, a crossroads of international cuisine, Irish pubs and local Belgian bars. On the corner of the two streets sits a cluster of similar Italian restaurants, all of which offer decent, good-value food. There's place de Luxembourg, a square overshadowed by the giant glass conservatories of the parliament building and surrounded by cafés, pubs and restaurants. Finally, there's place Jourdan, a square that hosts a market on Sunday mornings and a fine range of mainly Belgian places on a more permanent basis. The EU Quarter is busy at lunchtimes, but at night, once the workers have headed home, it's considerably calmer.

Restaurants

Belgian & French

L'Atelier Européen

28 rue Franklin (02 734 91 40). Métro Schuman.
Meals served noon-2.30pm, 7-10pm Mon-Fri.
Average €€. **Credit** AmEx, DC, MC, V.
Once upon a time, coaches would have driven through the big old doors and into the courtyard here, allowing the owners of the grand house to alight before continuing through to the coach house and stables at the back. No more. After a spell as artist's studios – the light and airy feel would have been perfect for the role, as would the

whitewashed walls – it's now a restaurant serving a menu that mixes Belgian and French dishes with a concentration of fish; choose from a starter or a main course buffet. The reasonable prices have helped make it a lively place, and it's proved especially popular with large groups. The courtyard, surrounded by climbing plants, is stunning in summer.

Au Bain-Marie

46 rue Breydel (02 280 48 88). Métro Schuman.
Meals served noon-3pm Mon-Fri. **Average** €€.
Credit AmEx, DC, MC, V.
A stylish café-restaurant, modern and minimalist, in the heart of the EU Quarter that serves healthy French-style basics. Greys are the running colour theme, providing a cool background for the office workers who drop in here for an informal lunch and catch-up with friends. Clothless tables lend the café feel, but the food moves it up in the genre stakes. A speciality here is a crisp-based pissaladière, a tart of caramelised onions and olives from Nice. Served with a huge salad, it's more than enough to keep you going for the afternoon. Also on offer are home-made quiches, both vegetarian and meaty, including a classic quiche Lorraine and a niçoise-style with tuna. The rear garden gets packed in summer.

Au Charlot

1 rue Froissart (02 230 33 28). Métro Schuman.
Meals served 11.30am-3pm Mon-Fri. **Average** €€€.
Credit AmEx, DC, MC, V.

Au Charlot

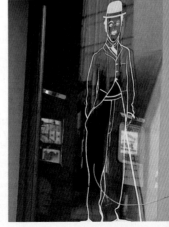

This brasserie was named in homage to Charlie Chaplin. Signage apart, though, there's no real sign of him within the old-fashioned, warm and cosy interior, which carries a lived-in, flea-market-y and thoroughly informal feel. Hordes of Euro-workers flock in every lunchtime, yet the place copes admirably; the owners are friendly and by now well accustomed to serving a multilingual crowd. Slabs of steak with sauce à choix, the requisite mussels, great bowls of crunchy chips and a mean sea bass sum up the traditional Belgian kitchen.

Chez Moi ★

66 rue du Luxembourg (02 280 26 66). Métro Trône.
Meals served noon-3pm, 7-11pm Mon-Fri. **Average** €.
Credit AmEx, MC, V.

Chez Moi is a real favourite in the European quarter. If you visit at lunchtime, you can pretend to be a Eurocrat: every nationality heads here, though English is the common language. Even better, everyone seems to speak louder than is absolutely necessary, and the conversation is ripe for overhearing if you're of a nosy or curious disposition. While you're listening to the latest developments in Fisheries, order some seared scallops in balsamic vinegar; if you're within listening range of a discussion of the Common Agricultural Policy, chow down on rare fillet steaks or lamb fillet with flageolets. The restaurant, which isn't especially large, is spread over two floors with a look heavily reliant on dark wood and whitewashed wall; very in, very now and very good.

L'Esprit de Sel Brasserie

52-54 place Jourdan (02 230 60 40). Métro Maalbeek.
Meals served noon-midnight daily. **Average** €€.
Credit MC, V.

An explanation is necessary. Two restaurants next door to each other, the mothership and her baby brasserie. The former was formerly L'Esprit de Sel, the latter L'Esprit de Sel Brasserie, but then the owners knocked a hole between the two and decided to place them both under one name. The two rooms still have different decor (you can specify your choice when you book): mama is done out in cool velour tones with a stunning Murano glass chandelier, while her lad is dressed in wood, marble and copper. But the food is the same throughout – there's a heavily Belgian influence down the menu, from chicken and chips through to rabbit in beer and horse steak – and whichever side of the divide you dine, you'll find a clientele made up of artistes, free-thinkers and the occasional celebrity.

Symphony ★

Renaissance Hotel, 19 rue du Parnasse (02 505 25 81).
Bus 95, 96. **Meals served** noon-2pm, 6.30-10pm daily.
Average €€€. **Credit** AmEx, DC, MC, V.

One of the best bakers in town is **Au Vatel** (27 place Jourdan). Fantastic bread, cakes and biscuits, and all served 24 hours daily to stave off those late-night munchies.

Chez Moi. *See p87.*

Its location opposite the European Parliament means that this Michelin-starred hotel is often used by the great and good, and its flagship restaurant is every bit as upscale as you might expect. Symphony briefly went under the name Nico Central, but since Mr Ladenis pulled out, Belgian chef Philippe Le Comte has taken the place over and continued to cook using his inspiration: the menu contains assorted fabulous creations containing wild mushrooms, foie gras and the like. Like the food, the decor is contemporary and clean, but you always know you're in a hotel. Still, try not to let it put you off: both food and service here are first class.

International

Balthazar
63 rue Archimède (02 742 06 00). Métro Schuman.
Meals served noon-2.30pm, 7-10.30pm Mon-Fri; 6-11pm Sat. **Average** €€. **Credit** AmEx, MC, V.
East meets west over at Balthazar, both in its minimalist decor and its fusion cooking. This stylish restaurant serves clean combinations of French classics jazzed up with the likes of ginger and lemongrass and exquisitely presented with drizzles of this and dots of that; indeed, with its Pacific Rim feel, it wouldn't seem

Go to colourful deli **Le Fermier** (59 rue Archimède) for the Italian job: cooked meats, oils, vinegars and fresh pasta.

terribly out of place in California. Dining here can be a pleasingly private affair, with high-backed banquettes giving tables a safe, secluded feel. However, during the summer months, many prefer to venture out back to the grand garden.

Le Cosmopolitie

36 avenue de Cortenberg (02 230 20 95). Métro Schuman. **Meals served** 11.30am-3pm (hot), 3-6pm (cold) Mon-Fri. **Average** €€. **Credit** MC, V.

The huge windows of this corner-plot landmark draw the eyes of the passing pedestrians into the white wood and stainless steel interior, done out with linen director's chairs. Geographically, Le Cosmopolitie sits at the heart of the major European institutions, and makes a great option for a power lunch or a catch-up gossip with friends. The extensive, modernist menu gives pride of place to salads, and what mighty salads they are; with ingredients ranging from giant fresh prawns to foie gras and figs, they're designed to look good and feed you well, being on the pleasant side of generous.

Le Jardin d'Espagne

65-67 rue Archimède (02 736 34 49). Métro Schuman. **Meals served** noon-2.30pm, 7-9.30pm Mon-Fri; 7-9.30pm Sat. **Average** €€€. **Credit** AmEx, DC, MC, V.

Some swear by the authenticity of this famed Spanish restaurant in the EU Quarter, while others bemoan its impersonal, indifferent staff. Certainly, it's not helped by its location on a street of unarguably fine eateries, though Le Jardin d'Espagne is the only one offering the real Spanish experience (tapas, paella, grilled meats, prawns). The chef has seemingly been here forever and regularly cooks for Spanish Embassy functions, so it can't be too bad. Downstairs, there's a more informal tapas bar, perfect for a quick glass of something red and a little nibble of something filling.

La Maison de la Pizza

130 rue de Trèves (02 230 90 80). Métro Trône/bus 20, 21. **Meals served** noon-2.30pm Mon-Fri. **Average** €. **Credit** AmEx, MC, V.

As you might expect from its plain-as-day name, La Maison de la Pizza is nothing special to look at: it's a standard little Italian pizzeria, of the type you'll find in many major cities across the planet. Still, don't be deceived by appearances, for the pizzas – baked in a wood-burning oven – have the thinnest bases known to man, and come immaculately prepared. You can eat them in or take them away, but be warned: if you decide to stay here to chow down, you may find the air can be thick with smoke. Not from the oven, mind, but from the perpetually burning ciggies smoked by other diners.

Mi-Figue Mi-Raisin

71 rue Archimède (02 734 24 84). Métro Schuman. **Meals served** 8am-7pm Mon-Fri. **Average** €. **No credit cards**.

Mi-Figue Mi-Raisin describes itself as a bakery and pâtisserie, but it's really just being unduly modest about what it offers. Inside the fantastic old townhouse that houses it, a set of stained-glass windows reminds you that the fig and grape represent femininity and virility. The small tables are invariably full as breakfast gives way to lunch, and the dishes of choice switch from pastries and almond croissants to chunky sandwiches, soups and salads. Everything served here is organic, and while it's not an exclusively vegetarian eatery, the menu is split roughly 50/50 between meaty dishes and veggie-friendly fodder. Still, it's clear that what you're getting is the finest organic food at decently inorganic prices.

Mi-Tango

31 rue du Spa (02 230 99 95). Métro Arts-Loi. **Meals served** noon-3pm, 7-10.30pm Mon-Fri. **Average** €€. **Credit** AmEx, DC, MC, V.

What was once a sandwich bar is now a tiny, cosy little Italian restaurant run by a wonderful Argentinian named Walter, who flits around the tables seeing to the every

Maison Antoine, in the middle of place Jourdan, is the best friterie in town, offering perfect cones of double-fried chips with a choice of over 20 sauces. Take them to **Chez Bernard** (*see p94*) for a napkin and a beer list.

Rue Franklin

need of his sizeable coterie of regulars. The speciality of the house is the piadina: the same idea as pizza, but with a base resembling fried filo pastry. However, in the evenings, the menu becomes more pasta-led, stretching its wings to such original sauces as ricotta and lemon ravioli with curry cream and saffron sauce. Friday night is piano night, when the place really camps it up. It's tiny, too, so do try and book.

Pappa e Citti ★
18 rue Franklin (02 732 61 10). Métro Schuman.
Meals served noon-2.30pm, 7-10pm Mon-Fri.
Average €€€. **Credit** AmEx, DC, MC, V.
Pappa e Citti stands out above the pack of Italian restaurants at the bottom end of rue Franklin. Chiefly, it's because the menu's mostly Sardinian. Fish figures prominently on the menu and the day's catch can be simply grilled or dressed in a tomato and wine-based sauce. Another speciality of the region and of the house are dried fish eggs; powerful and intense in flavour, they're used as a garnish on the richly flavoured food. The restaurant's pasta is made on the premises. Set in a small townhouse with a garden for summer dining, Pappa e Citti is a homely sort of place, so much so that the tank of lobsters fits in like a tropical fish tank. It's also much loved by EU officials: one Commissioner himself considers it his local.

Le Rocher Fleuri ★
19 rue Franklin (02 735 00 21). Métro Schuman.
Meals served noon-3pm, 6.30-11pm Mon-Fri.
Average €. **Credit** AmEx, MC, V.
This Oriental restaurant is not just a real star: it's also owned by one. Her name is Madame Lâm Thi Thiêu Quang, and her CV includes a degree in chemical

engineering, stints as a tightrope walker and a magician, and details of her current job as a chef extraordinaire. Of an evening, Madame stands in the thick of the action at her kitsch empire, clad in a glaring gold and pink silk dress and regally surveying the action that surrounds her. But then she gets down to cooking, and what brilliant cooking it is: fish curries, black ducks, roaringly hot chilli soups, stir-fries and steam-ups. There's a good-value buffet option (€12.95, or €21.95 including wine), though it's only available at lunchtimes and on Friday night.

Takesushi ★

21 boulevard Charlemagne (02 230 56 27). Métro Maalbeek or Schuman. **Meals served** noon-2.30pm, 7-10.30pm Mon-Fri; 6-10.30pm Sun. **Average** €€€. **Credit** AmEx, MC, V.

The name of this restaurant sounds like a whisper, which perfectly sums up the quiet, cool atmosphere in what is – perhaps surprisingly – one of the only Japanese places in the area. Takesushi caters for the European institution crowd, and plays to their egos by treating them like demi-gods with a formality that borders on the worshipful. It won't work, fellas: there's no way Japan

A breath of fetid Eire

In most cities, Irish theme bars are a blight as monolithically ugly as any hamburger or coffee chain: the cod Celtic paraphernalia, the miled signpost to Kilkenny, the overpriced stew. Brussels' are as unsightly as any other, but in the context of the city's displaced international community plonked in one strange spot, they play a slightly different role. Scattered around Schuman, the vast steel-and-glass grindstone for the institutionalised EU workforce, are a host of Irish hostelries that dominate the social whirl. Although only four swift metro stops from the grime of Gare Centrale,

Schuman exists in its own separate bubble, an island of Eurocracy annexed to Brussels.

Elsewhere in Europe, Irish bars tend to be hulking meat markets set up in central parts of town, spilling over on rugby Saturdays and Premiership Sundays; in Eastern Europe, they're pick-up joints for native floozettes to find the comfortably-off yet lonely home counties man of their dreams. Friday nights see a flurry of activity in the ladies' loos, Miss Slovakias of 2003 padding their bras to net the Mr Caterhams of 1983. Moscow's lary expat dive the Hungry Duck became so outrageous, the Duma itself forced its closure.

will be allowed to join the EU. Regardless, the place wins bonus points for its perfect, precise sashimi and its brilliantly light teriyaki. Indeed, right down the menu, the food is delicate and often seriously wonderful, but don't come here for a boisterous night out.

Bars

Bok & Dragon

189 rue du Noyer (02 733 39 66). Métro Schuman/ bus 21, 28. **Open** 11am-late daily. **No credit cards**. Located on the edge of the EU Quarter and attracting the younger element of its diasporic community, this tidy operation is named to represent the joint South African and Welsh management who run it. Locals still use the bar, so events such as the invasion of Scotland's tartan army into Brussels generate incongruous and friendly scenes of drunken bekilted Jocks dancing around bemused old ladies delighted with such rare and close attention. On an average night, the sons and daughters of balding Eurocrats meet to compare career paths, shoot pool and sink beers.

EU Quarter

In Schuman, Irish bars are locals, used by these strangely misplaced drinkers to natter, network and, on specific occasions, neck. Weekday nights they heave; weekends, they act as liferafts for expats stranded in town until Monday. On scheduled stagiaire evenings, each pub in turn invites fresh, young EU interns to imbibe cheaply and see where two litres of underpriced Breezer can lead. Voyeurs can mark their calendar by the posters put up in each bar promoting the next Tuesday's hedonistic onslaught.

The bars themselves are much of a muchness. The **Wild Geese** (2 avenue Livingstone, 02 230 19 90) is the most brazen; **Kitty O'Shea's** (boulevard Charlemagne, 02 230 78 75) is more middle-aged. The **Hairy Canary** (12 rue Archimède, 02 280 05 09) sports Anglophile touches, such as Walker's crisps and faux Victoriana; down the road, the **James Joyce** (34 rue Archimède, 02 230 98 94) answers back with equal volumes of Celtic kitsch, trumping it with live twiddly music on alternate weeks. On weekends, the expat drones swap hives to the centrally located **O'Reilly's** (1 place de la Bourse, 02 552 04 80), to curse or cheer on United after a Sunday roast.

Anarkali
Curry in a hurry. *See p105.*

L'Atelier Européen
Through the stable door. *See p85.*

Les Perles de Pluie
Thai chi-chi. *See p108.*

Le Rocher Fleuri
Kitsch in sync. *See p91.*

EU Quarter

Chez Bernard
47 place Jourdan (02 230 22 38). Métro Maelbeek or Schuman. **Open** 6.30am-1am daily. **No credit cards**.
An oasis of authentic Belgarama in a sea of faceless Eurocracy, Chez Bernard comprises a traditional mirrored beer hall and an incongruous conservatory. The latter may have been constructed in deference to the occasional bureaucrat drinker, who'd occasionally like to dip his toes into the local waters without having to suffer the inconvenience of venturing into town to do so. In any case, most of the cigarette smoke misting up the mirrors is genuine, Bedouine Belga. Complementing the ciggies is l'essence de frites, the smell of chips and mayonnaise brought in from the famous Maison Antoine frites stall opposite. No need for cup-a-soup or croque monsieur Chez Bernard; buy your cone of chips over the road, bring them here and enjoy over a beer. No corkage charge, napkins provided with pleasure.

Fat Boy's
5 place du Luxembourg (02 511 32 66/www.fat-boys.com). Métro Trône. **Open** 10.30am-late daily. **Credit** MC, V.
Fat Boy's is Brussels' main expatriate sports bar, conveniently set in the considerable shadow of the European Parliament. Although it's American in style, Brits flock here in droves to spend beery Sunday afternoons gawping moronically at slick, muddy Premiership action and scoffing their way through the meaty menu of ribs and burgers. Fat Boy's improves when the post-work crowd fills its long interior, spilling out onto the terrace in summer. By dusk of a Friday, most have had the good sense to escape, thus avoiding the woeful live R&B and Celtic drivel somehow conceived as a regular attraction.

For a hot, gungy panini, drop into **Le Sfizio** (22-24 rue Archimède), where you can also get a frighteningly fresh daily selection of veggies in olive oil.

Ixelles

Ixelles

Ixelles is a sprawling commune that has eating and drinking hot-spots right across it. The main arterial avenue Louise is the most upmarket thoroughfare; place du Châtelain is its young, trendy satellite, while café-covered place St-Boniface has become popular with thirtysomethings. There's also the Matongé, peopled by Brussels' African population and home to soul food eateries, exotic delis and crazy bars. And down by Ixelles Ponds is another clutch of quality restaurants, frequented by wealthies after serious cooking. Ixelles is a true melting-pot of class, culture and cuisine, a locale that becomes more glamorous – and dear – as it moves away from the city centre.

Restaurants

Belgian & French

L'Amadeus
13 rue Veydt (02 538 34 27). Tram 91, 92.
Meals served 6.30pm-midnight Tue-Thur; 6.30pm-12.30am Fri, Sat; 10am-2.30pm, 6.30pm-midnight Sun. **Average** €€€. **Credit** AmEx, MC, V.

Ixelles

Chez Marie. *See p101.*

Ixelles

The best — Candlelit dinners

L'Amadeus
Not your average romantic ambience. *See p97.*

Le Cap Sablon
If the cap fits... *See p73.*

Chez Moi
Argentian goes Italian in the EU. *See p90.*

Divino
Talking Italian. *See p63.*

Ma Folle de Soeur
Sisters are doin' it for themselves. *See p129.*

Le Petit Boxeur
Packs a punch. *See p59.*

La Table d'Abbaye
Get the Abbaye habit. *See p107.*

Ixelles

Note, first of all, the opening times: this is one of the few restaurants in Brussels where you're welcome late at night. Certainly, the Ixelles set take full advantage of the extended opening, though they're usually joined by people stopping in for a bite on their way home from a night downtown. Don't expect a peaceful supper: L'Amadeus pulses with noise and activity as groups of hungries tuck into brasserie-type goodies such as grilled goat's cheese with honey. The building in which it's housed used to be Rodin's workshop, but today, marble splinters have given way to candlelit darkness and cosy little snug tables. All a bit of an adventure.

Aux Beaumes de Venise ★

62 rue Darwin (02 343 82 93). Tram 91, 92.
Meals served noon-2pm, 7-10pm Tue-Sat.
Average €€€. **Credit** AmEx, MC, V.
There's something Parisian about this elegant, sophisticated restaurant; or, at least, that's what they'd like you to think. The decor is grand and sumptuous, although – a welcome surprise, this – both clientele and staff are totally unpretentious. Aux Beaumes de Venise's aim is to prepare the highest quality French cuisine – lick those lips at the thought of langoustines on potatoes with black truffle – in friendly, accessible surroundings, and it's one at which they succeed. A set menu with four

LE FILS DE JULES
RÉSOLUMENT BASQUE ET LANDAIS

choices for each course (€35) makes it a more affordable option than it might otherwise be; certainly, you'd pay double in the French capital.

Café Camille

559 chaussée de Waterloo (02 345 96 43). Bus 37, 38, 60. **Meals served** 11am-2.30pm, 7-11pm Mon-Fri; 7-11pm Sat, Sun. **Average** €€€. **Credit** AmEx, DC, MC, V.

This fine little place doesn't figure on most visitors' itineraries simply because it's well off the beaten tourist track. But it's worth the not inconsiderable diversion for the food, classic French cooking with a twist: sole with saffron, seafood brioche, duck breast with mango and some rather stunning goat's cheese rolled in pine nuts. During lunchtimes, you'll find suits and their expense accounts chowing down, but in the evenings, local residents return again and again, receiving a warm welcome every time. A small gravel garden gives a dining-at-home feel in the warmer months.

Canterbury

2 avenue de l'Hippodrome (02 646 83 93). Tram 71, 81, 82. **Meals served** noon-11.30pm Mon-Sat. **Average** €€€. **Credit** MC, V.

Canterbury is one of those brasseries that appeal to just about everyone from ladies with poodles to business suits. Though the menu is largely based around Belgian faves such as waterzooi and steak with sauce, it also introduces novelties: try its own weird take on fish and chips ('à la Liverpool', they reckon). To be honest, Canterbury is all a bit of a mess; it's hectic and loud, staffed by frantic waiters who have to dodge the dog bowls on the floor. Still, if it's character you're after, this place has it in spades.

Chez Marie ★

40 rue Alphonse de Witte (02 644 30 31). Tram 81, 82/bus 71. **Meals served** noon-2.30pm, 7.30-10.30pm Tue-Fri; 7.30-10.30pm Sat. **Average** €€€€. **Credit** AmEx, MC, V.

If you go down to the ponds today, you're sure of a big surprise. This unassuming little restaurant, tucked round the corner from the ponds in an unassuming little street, bears one of the most recent Michelin stars to arrive in Belgium. It was won by Lilian Devaux, a bright young French chef who has created a menu of classics with modern twists (including, in a tongue-in-cheek nod to 21st-century commercialism, a Michelin-starred burger). Devaux imports the majority of her produce from France, and top-quality stuff it is too: seafood from Brittany, chickens from Bresse, ducks from the south-west. The extensive wine list is overseen by Canadian sommelier Daniel Marcil. The decor is homely, all checked materials and wood panelling, and the atmosphere as cosy as the small size of the restaurant suggests it should be (only around 40 covers, so booking essential).

Le Fils de Jules ★

35 rue du Page (02 534 00 57). Tram 81, 82, 91, 92.
Meals served noon-2.30pm, 7-11pm Mon-Thur; 7-11pm Fri-Sun. **Average** €€€. **Credit** AmEx, DC, MC, V.
Come to the heart of Trendsville and sit down to dine with the well-heeled set, who've come to Le Fils de Jules in search of the authentic French foodie experience. This restaurant, whose menu is set in the border region of the Landais and Basque region, doesn't disappoint; plates heavily laden with luscious duck products, chunks of fish, thick lentils and salardais potatoes leave most diners more than satisfied. The wine list merits special mention, too, not least for its unintelligible local-language labels (Txacoli, for example). Sunday evenings are jollied along by a great value set menu (€23), but the restaurant, whose decor is an odd mix of art deco and part naffo, buzzes most of the time.

Le Garde-Manger

151 rue Washington (02 346 68 29). Tram 93, 94.
Meals served noon-3pm, 6-10.30pm Mon, Wed-Sat. **Average** €€€. **Credit** AmEx, DC, MC, V.
This sophisticated, candlelit brasserie is the archetype of a neighbourhood bar and restaurant. Locals drop by for a drink in the front room, or to sit at the bar and tuck in if they're eating alone. The main room and the funky downstairs lounge bar are theatrical but calm, with original works of art creating a slightly bohemian ambience; taupe, aubergine and flickering candles are the names of the game. The diverse menu offers some intriguing surprises, such as duck breast in lavender sauce. The busy, buzzy summer terrace will keep you gossiping until dark, not least with Irish Brian (out front) and Belgian Claude (in the kitchen) making all-comers feel welcome.

Le Grain de Sel

9 chaussée de Vleurgat (02 648 18 58). Tram 81, 82/ bus 71. **Meals served** noon-2pm, 7.30-10pm Tue-Fri; 7.30-10pm Sat. **Average** €. **Credit** MC, V.
Grégory Yarm brings his dear old Portuguese gran's influence into his French cooking at this pretty little restaurant right by the ponds. It's a homely place, with a rose garden for summer dining and chandeliers inside. The food is as authentically home-cooked as you'll find in a professional operation; certainly, in such strongly flavoured dishes as tomato with goat's cheese, and tartare of salmon with horseradish, it appears to owe little to textbook cheffery. Le Grain de Sel has regular diners in

Join the ladies who lunch at **Gourmand Gaillard** (192 chaussée de Vleurgat) for a slice of quiche or some fantastically sticky tarts and cakes.

Ixelles

Market value

As in most other European cities, supermarkets across Belgium offer more or less every fruit, vegetable and lump of meat known to man. However, also as in most other European cities, a local supermarket's still just a supermarket: convenient, good value and infinitely less enjoyable than buying a wrap of cheese from a friendly granny-farmer up from the country for market day.

Markets in Brussels generally fall into two broad categories. First, there are the large, general, multicultural markets where you can buy anything from a toothbrush to a wardrobe. Then, there are the smaller community markets where food is the guiding principle. Of the first category, the two largest take place on Sunday mornings to the south of the city.

The **Midi Market** (métro Gare du Midi) sets up in the streets and arches around the Gare du Midi. It's also known as the Mediterranean market as the majority of stall-holders are of north African origin, something reflected in the style and content of the goods. Among them are mountains of olives, loose almonds and walnuts, bunches of herbs, and hunks of fish and meat, but it's the vegetables that win out: sold in bulk, they run the range from apples to mangoes. Nearby, in the expansive covered ex-abattoir of **Anderlecht** (métro Clemenceau), the city's other big market offers a similar range of food to Midi.

However, it is to the weekly borough markets that most Bruxellois head to buy specific foods. Among the best of them is the Wednesday afternoon market on **place du Châtelain** in Ixelles (tram 93, 94), and the Sunday morning market on **place Jourdain** in Etterbeek (métro Maelbeek). Stalls tend to be modern refrigerated vans with pull-down fronts that expose glass counters, in which are displayed specialist cheeses, Italian deli foods, fresh bakery goods and assorted fruit and veg.

much the same way as a pub would have drinkers. But don't assume you'll be treated like an outsider: the service is as charming as can be, and only adds to the feeling that you've actually been invited to someone's home for dinner.

Mange Ta Soupe
7 rue de la Tulipe (02 512 14 12). Bus 54, 71.
Meals served 11.30am-3pm Mon-Sat. **Average** €.
No credit cards.
'Eat your soup or you won't get any afters!' Childhood memories of miserable lunches conjured up by such exhortations will soon give way to relief as you realise

the name is just a joke, albeit one that accurately reflects
the content of its menu. Mange Ta Soupe is all about
serious bowls of the stuff, thick and home-made and
served with large hunks of bread. If it doesn't set you on
the straight and narrow for the afternoon ahead, nothing
will, whether you eat it here or take it away. Oh, and if
you're good boys and girls, there are desserts and
cheeses to scoff afterwards.

La Quincaillerie

45 rue du Page (02 538 25 53). Tram 81, 82.
Meals served noon-2.30pm, 7pm-midnight Mon-Fri;
7pm-midnight Sat, Sun. **Average** €€€. **Credit** AmEx,
DC, MC, V.
This old ironmonger's shop, complete with giant clock,
wooden drawers for holding nails and screws and cast-
iron gallery, is a marvel of a bygone era. However, it's
also a present-day favourite, a perennially packed place-
to-be-seen. Its popularity is entirely down to the food,
undeniably impressive French brasserie fare with an
especially notable seafood bar. However, grit your teeth
while ordering, as the service is rather abrupt and
impersonal. Maybe its regulars like to be considered as
something more special.

Raconte-Moi des Salades

19 place du Châtelain (02 534 27 27). Tram 93, 94.
Meals served noon-2.30pm, 7-11pm Mon-Sat.
Average €€. **Credit** MC, V.

The menu at this oh-so-trendy spot bang on the square is a good combination of vegetarian and carnivorous (among the standouts is grilled beef with rosemary on roquette and parmesan). Whatever your inclinations, though, you can rely on getting a goodly salad with whatever you order. Inside, the decor is warm and somewhat colonial with a slight Indian edge; outside sits a decent terrace, open during the summer. But regardless of whether you're sitting outside or in, the atmosphere is relaxed and go-with-the-flow. A real bonus are the prices, which remain reasonable for this largely upmarket part of Ixelles that's home to many more expensive spots.

Saint Boniface

9 rue St-Boniface (02 511 53 66). Métro Porte de Namur/bus 71. **Meals served** noon-2.30pm, 7-10pm Mon-Thur; noon-2.30pm, 7-11pm Sat. **Average** €€. **Credit** AmEx, MC, V.

This little eatery sits proudly among a slew of far trendier restaurants in this gastronome's corner of Brussels, entirely unashamed of its red-and-white checks, its mock oil lamplights and its old posters. Saint Boniface is confident of its south-western France heritage, and rightly so, serving as it does the best of the region with a frill-free flourish. By its nature, the food is sturdy, with duck, goose, lamb and juicy lentils from Puy. Madame is similarly no-nonsense, and has pinned up signs forbidding mobile phones. Quite right too, since you really don't want to be distracted from the food at this particular geographical time warp; although it only opened in 1987, it feels as if Périgord invaded and took root in another era. Wonderful.

Toucan

1 avenue Louis Lepoutre (02 345 30 17). Tram 91, 92.
Meals served noon-11pm Mon-Fri; noon-11.30pm Sat, Sun. **Average** €€€. **Credit** AmEx, DC, MC, V.
This busy brasserie is set in a magnificent townhouse, and has been designed with the style triallers in mind: the floors are clean and sleek, and the walls are punctuated by colourful pictures and outrageous designer lighting. Chef Jean-Pierre Gascouin rustles up a classic Belgian-French mix with leanings towards Italy in a flurry of parmesan shavings. Among the highlights is the AAAAA Andouillet, a banger with guts (literally), and the lighter mille-feuille of tuna with a fondue of leek. It's all a little upmarket and precise, but the food on offer has rapidly become the casual subject of plentiful raves from the chattering classes.

La Truffe Noire ★

12 boulevard de la Cambre (02 640 44 22). Tram 93, 94.
Meals served noon-2.30pm, 7-9.30pm Mon-Fri; 7-9.30pm Sat. **Average** €€€€€. **Credit** AmEx, DC, MC, V.
Truffles with everything and a Michelin star: what else needs to be said? Not much, save that La Truffe Noire is friendly and totally unpretentious, that chef Luigi Ciciriello is passionate about his black diamonds, and that the dining room cuddles up to you with a soft, comforting embrace. The prices here mean that it's usually only used for special celebrations or business meetings, but hell, bresse squab with norcia truffles, sautéd potatoes and mushrooms with foie gras and périgourdine sauce shouldn't be the kind of food on which you munch casually twice a week. Yum.

De la Vigne à l'Assiette

51 rue de la Longue Haie (02 647 68 03). Métro Louise.
Meals served noon-2pm, 7-11.30pm Tue-Fri; 7-11.30pm Sat. **Average** €. **Credit** AmEx, MC, V.
De la Vigne à l'Assiette is a real star of a restaurant. It sits alone in a long, characterless residential street, but its windows throw a glow from afar; once inside, the scrubbed wooden chairs and globe lamps give the place the feel of a brasserie. However, the menu and outstanding wine list is much more than that, with the French-influenced food spiced up with worldly influences and appealing to the young, professional crowd who inhabit the seemingly irresistible 1050 postcode district. Run by two young Belgians, it has a relaxed and informal atmosphere, suitable for both power business lunches and lovers' trysts (though not both at once).

Fish & seafood

Rouge Tomate

190 avenue Louise (02 647 70 44). Tram 93, 94.
Meals served noon-2.30pm, 6.30-11.30pm daily.
Average €€€. **Credit** AmEx, MC, V.

Fred Nicolay's empire has moved out of St-Géry and taken a firm hold in Ixelles. And how: never satisfied with half-measures, it's gallantly taken on one of the area's prime locations, a location that's drawn a happy crowd of trendies to the place. As the name suggests, it's a bright and brash place, with a fish-heavy menu that offers a new and vibrant take on Belgian cooking. Rouge Tomate also offers a great choice for vegetarians, a sure sign that Nicolay has recognised the demographics of the neighbourhood. Yet, in keeping with his other outlets, his staff remain laid back and relaxed, maintaining a dead cool image that only succeeds in boring the diner.

La Table d'Abbaye

62 rue du Belle-Vue (02 646 33 95). Tram 93, 94. **Meals served** noon-2.30pm, 6.30-10.30pm Mon-Fri; 6.30-10.30pm Sat. **Average** €€€. **Credit** AmEx, DC, MC, V.

What a romantic little place this is: set in a lovely old townhouse, the decor is all swags and frills, with a running theme of blue and yellow. The garden in the summer is one of the best in the city, a candlelit haven dripping with gauze. The food's not cheap, but then you are getting classic fish dishes in classic French sauces, a fine wine list and largely impeccable service that runs on railway tracks. As long as everything goes to plan, that is: when we dined there, a spilt glass of red wine sent staff into a confused flurry. It clashed with the colour scheme, see?

International

Anarkali

33 rue du Longue Vie (02 513 02 05). Métro Porte de Namur. **Meals served** noon-2.30pm, 6pm-midnight daily. **Average** €. **Credit** AmEx, DC, MC, V.

Anarkali used to be a run-of-the-mill Indian restaurant until the owners decided to go buffet-style. As the crowds waiting for a table prove almost nightly, it was an inspired idea. Of course, such popularity probably has more than a little to do with the €13 set price, which includes everything from nan breads to coffee and dessert. However, those who can't bear the thought of chafing dishes and spirit burners should note that Anarkali is sensible about its buffet, restricting the dishes to a realistic number and making sure that the food is

Combine a passion for art with a passion for wine at **Le Chai de Marianne** (58 rue du Page). There are wine tastings every Saturday, and exhibitions of work by local artists year-round.

Ixelles

The next generation

In 1983, a young chef named Stefaan Couttenye opened Hommelhof, a restaurant in Watou. With it, he kick-started a new trend in Belgian cuisine. Couttenye found ancient local recipes that employed plenty of Belgian beer and updated them to make them lighter. Rather than using a whole bottle of dark brown tripel to flavour a rabbit terrine, he modified the balance of ingredients to allow other flavours to make their presence felt. In so doing, Couttenye helped define what's now regarded as modern Belgian cuisine, his ideas taken on board by the old brigade but pioneered by the young.

Taking after the French tradition, Belgian cooking has always relied on the classic master-apprenticeship relationship, as typified by Pierre Wynants and son-in-law Lionel Rigolet at **Comme Chez Soi** (see p27). However, these days Wynants relies on the younger *chef-supreme* to continue and develop the restaurant's three-star excellence, appealing to a new generation of diners.

Another example of hand-me-down excellence is Tom Decroos, who worked for a spell under Michelin-winner Yves Mattagne at the **Sea Grill** (see p34). Decroos has moved on to open his own seafood restaurant, **Vismet** (see p53), and to develop his own modern style of preparation that offers a nod to classic sauces but introduces minimalist themes that reflect the tastes of Brussels' younger diners.

wet, not dry and crusty round the edges. It all seems to disappear quickly enough, mind you, which helps to ensure its freshness.

Cose Cosi

16 chaussée de Wavre (02 512 11 71). Métro Porte de Namur. **Meals served** noon-3pm, 6-11.30pm Mon-Thur, Sun; noon-3pm, 6pm-midnight Fri, Sat. **Average** €€.
Credit AmEx, MC, V.

From the outside, the rambling Cose Cosi is clearly Italian, but once inside, you'll find zebra skins, antelope heads and other African artefacts staring you in the face. It only gets stranger from here: hang around long enough and you'll see the chef emerge from the kitchen to join the pianist in a serenade… Sorry, where were we? The food, you say? Simple enough: the menu is full of Italian staples, such as pizzas, pastas, grilled meats and the ubiquitous tricolore. But as you examine the options, try not to be too unnerved by the Zulu warrior mask casting a beady eye over you.

The new breed of chefs prefer their dishes lighter, yet without ignoring some basic French rules of cooking. Among them are Frédéric Salpetier, who produces an elegant, considered cuisine at **Le Cabri** in the Ardennes (route du Hérou 45, Nadrin, 084 44 41 85). Based on the region's game and fish, his cooking insists on a lighter touch with butter, cream and alcohol, allowing flavours such as green pepper to bite through.

Such country cooking has filtered its way into the cities, influencing such rising stars as Stéphane Charlier, whose style of French cooking at **La Salicornne** (rue Pierre Broodcoorens 41, La Hulpe, 02 654 01 71) is considered among the best of the new classic cuisine. World influences creep in, too, and the new chef ignores them at his peril: Carlo Didden at **Kleine Zavel** in Antwerp (*see p175*), who experiments with Asian spices and innovative presentation styles, is a case in point.

Yet the classics continue to inspire and dominate, and new cross-border experiments have begun. Brussels' brightest star is Lilian Devaux, a Française in Belgium, who won her first Michelin star last year at the tiny **Chez Marie** (*see p101*). With one eye on nostalgia, occasionally winking at regional French tradition, Devaux has led the way in breaking boundaries in this country where only seven per cent of chefs are women.

Le Deuxième Element

7 rue St-Boniface (02 502 00 28). Métro Porte de Namur. **Meals served** noon-2.30pm, 7-11pm Mon-Fri; 7-11pm Sat, Sun. **Average** €€. **Credit** AmEx, DC, MC, V.

Le Deuxième Element sits perfectly among the neighbouring trendies of the St-Boniface neighbourhood. There's not a hint of a Buddha or a fluorescent photo of a floating market in sight in the stylish interior: rather, the decor is Philippe-style Starck-ness, all shiny metals and pinpoint lights, with a vast spacey mural filling one wall of the place. Those blessed with fertile imaginations may feel they're getting set to take flight to another planet, yet the food remains resolutely and comfortably Thai. There's been no unnecessary culinary messing with the requisite doses of coconut and lemongrass, nor have the fierce curries – made with whole chillies, they're quite a winter warmer – been noticeably toned down. It's a friendly place, too; quaff some of the by-the-metre spiced-up gin and go for it.

Cose Cosi. *See p108.*

es

Ixelles

es

Dolma ★

*329 chaussée d'Ixelles (02 649 89 81). Tram 81, 82/
bus 71.* **Meals served** noon-2pm, 7-9.30pm Mon-Sat.
Average €. Credit AmEx, DC, MC, V.

In this city of carnivores, Dolma stands out a mile as its
best vegetarian restaurant. There is a Buddhist feel as
you enter, though it's no theme park and the staff have
no pretensions other than to serve you with consistently
high-quality food. Dolma is run as a buffet and offers
bountiful salads, home-made quiches, pasta dishes and
irresistible desserts; it's also a place where even diehard
flesh-eaters can dine well and leave replete and contented.
Highly recommended.

EAT

103 rue de l'Aqueduc (02 537 22 90). Tram 81, 93, 94.
Meals served 9am-4pm Mon, Tue, Thur, Fri; 7-10pm
Wed; 10am-4pm Sat. **Average €. No credit cards**.

This trendy salad bar attracts the young, the slim and
the fit. Blackboards replace paper menus, which means
that every day begins with a clean slate depending on
what was in the market. Imaginative salads are the order
of the day, though the wholesome desserts – cake,
beautifully gluggy tarts – will remove any fitness feelgood factor you may have developed after choosing to
come here in the first place. Still, if it makes you feel
better, you can jog away with them instead: EAT also
offers a takeaway service.

L'Elément Terre

*465 chaussée de Waterloo (02 649 37 27). Tram 91,
92.* **Meals served** noon-2.30pm, 7-11.30pm Tue-Fri;
7-10.30pm Sat. **Average €€. Credit** MC, V.

The name's a pun. In its pure form it means 'earth, the
element'. But it also reads as *elémentaire*, as in
'elementary, my dear Watson'. Elementary is the name
of the game here, too: it's a small restaurant, whose quiet
and almost restrictive atmosphere seems to suggest that
vegetarians are all deeply earnest and deadly serious folk.
They're not, of course, but the excellent food still seems
to arrive wearing slippers and voices are rarely raised
above a whisper. The emphasis is on organic produce,
with pulses and grains as bases, blackened grilled
vegetables and pasta dishes. The 'discovery plate' is a
good way into the menu, offering a taste of this and that,
though in truth, you can't really go wrong with anything
on the menu.

Fellini

*32 place du Châtelain (02 534 47 49). Tram 81, 93,
94/bus 54.* **Meals served** 11.30am-3pm, 7-11.30pm
Mon, Tue, Thur-Sun; 7-11.30pm Wed. **Average €€.
Credit** AmEx, DC, MC, V.

Those
hard-to-find
Japanese
specialities
can be had
on the two
packed floors
of **Tagawa
Superstore**
(119
chaussée
de Vleurgat).

Kolya

[Lounge] [Restaurant] [Bar]

Ultra Lounge & Ultra Cosy
[Patio] [Terrasses] [Cigar Bar] [Garden]
French Cooking
World Wines
Jazz
Relax Atmosphere
FREE PARKING

World Cooking with
- monthly - **Globe Trotter Menu** [35 €]

Sunday Brunch
From noon till 4 PM [30 €]
Booking : 02/533.18.30

Kolya

[Lounge] [Restaurant] [Bar]
106, Chaussée de Charleroi - B-1060 Bruxelles
02/533.18.30 - info@kolya.be - www.kolya.be
Closed : Saturday noon & Sunday

Yes, it's named after Federico, the famed Italian film director, and no, the place isn't plastered with blown-up posters of his films. With its railway station aesthetic of wooden seats, metal pillars and painted murals, Fellini does look like something from *Brief Encounter*. But this ain't provincial England, and the decor is really a mysterious blend of Italian Renaissance and *Aladdin*. Within this setting you get classic Italian food prepared in the old style: ever-changing fresh pasta courses and a fall-off-the-bone osso bucco to write home to mama about.

Gioconda-Store

76 rue de l'Aqueduc (02 539 32 99). Tram 81, 82/ bus 54. **Meals served** noon-2.30pm, 7-10.30pm Mon-Sat. **Average** €€. **Credit** DC, MC, V.
Gioconda takes full advantage of its proximity to the hip Châtelain neighbourhood, and does well collecting custom from folk cruising the area for modern food in a friendly setting. The mains are standard Italian fare and the range of pasta dishes more than adequate, but the real star of the restaurant is undoubtedly the antipasti table, which groans under vegetables in olive oil, anchovies, salads and little slices of sausage. The 'store' part of the name comes from the fact that it's also an Italian deli, and sells all the bits and bobs you'll need for home cooking. The hunks of parmesan are particularly good.

Le Hasard des Choses

31 rue du Page (02 538 18 63). Tram 91, 92. **Meals served** noon-2.30pm, 7-10.30pm Mon-Thur; noon-2.30pm, 7-11pm Fri; 1-11pm Sat, Sun. **Average** €€. **Credit** V.
It was a toss-up as to in which category this rough 'n' ready bistro belonged. Le Hasard des Choses does serve some traditional Belgian dishes; carbonnade of beef is a favourite, and chicory pops up here and there in various incarnations. But the spin of the coin landed firmly on the Italian head for the restaurant's real speciality: home-made pastas, described as 'artisinale'. There's a studenty feel to the space, which is stocked with scrubbed tables and chairs, raw-brick walls and a forest of angle poise lamps. Still, it's as friendly and informal as can be and gets packed at more or less every opportunity.

Mont Liban

30-32 rue Livourne (02 537 71 31). Tram 91, 92, 93, 94. **Meals served** noon-3pm, 7-11pm Mon-Sat. **Average** €€. **Credit** AmEx, DC, MC, V.
Mont Liban is located in a smart part of town and attracts a smart set of customers. Chief among them are the expat Lebanese who come here to meet friends and family and chat for hours over the excellent plates of meze that just seem to keep on coming in perpetuity. Don't be alarmed if a great bowl of leaves arrives with whole cucumbers

and peppers; the idea is to pull them apart, then share and eat them. This is the joy of eating Lebanese-style: a shared no-rush experience with no fear of being under-fed. Mont Liban has proved itself a real winner in a fairly short time, its success doubtless helped along by the belly-dancer who wiggles in at weekends.

Ô Chinoise-Riz

94 rue de l'Aqueduc (02 534 91 08). Tram 91, 92.
Meals served noon-2.30pm, 6-11pm Mon-Fri; 6-11pm Sat, Sun. **Average** €. **Credit** MC, V.
This is a busy, busy restaurant. Sure, it's small for a Chinese restaurant, but its location means it attracts the young crowd of southern Ixelles, or those dropping down to the Châtelain area for a night out. And they'll find it an intimate spot once they get there, sitting down shoulder-to-shoulder with strangers all tucking heartily into perfectly prepared Chinese classics (the Peking duck, with its attendant pancakes, plum sauce and spring onions, is perfect). A step up from most of the ubiquitous lotus bloom-type restaurants around town.

Les Perles de Pluie ★

25 rue du Châtelain (02 649 67 23). Tram 93, 94.
Meals served noon-3pm, 7-11pm Tue-Fri; 7-11pm Sat.
Average €€. **Credit** MC, V.
Smart and even, perhaps, a little bit chi-chi, this Thai restaurant is famous for its Sunday buffet (€27). Understandably so, too: the food (by and large predictable chicken-in-Thai-curry-sauce variety, though there is a decent vegetarian section) is spread along huge tables and, uniquely for such a foodfest, includes most of the dishes from the restaurant's main menu. Only small portions are brought out at any one time which ensures freshness, essential for this style of speedy cooking. Some punters mistakenly call it a brunch, but it's not: the deal runs from lunchtime right through to late-night and there's nothing to stop you staying there the whole time. Just make sure you book.

La Porte des Indes ★

455 avenue Louise (02 647 86 51). Tram 93, 94.
Meals served noon-2.30pm, 7-10.30pm Mon-Fri; noon-2.30pm, 7-11.30pm Sat; 7-10.30pm Sun. **Average** €€€.
Credit AmEx, DC, MC, V.
An upmarket Indian restaurant in an upmarket location. Built into a 1920s townhouse, the style is Maharaja baroque (beware the potted palms and outsized flower displays which seem determined to catch you at every turn), the food finely presented, the service silently efficient. La Porte des Indes is regarded as the best place of its type in Brussels, something evidenced by the impeccably dressed diners who come here nightly for a

Ixelles

Vini e Antipasti. *See p116.*

gastronomic treat from India. Forget the ubiquitous curry: here you'll find such delights as sole fillets wrapped in mint chutney and a royal recipe from the court of Hyderabad, lamb cutlets marinaded in garam masala, ginger and lemon.

Vie Sauvage

12 rue de Naples (02 513 68 85). Métro Porte de Namur.
Meals served noon-2pm, 7-11pm Tue-Fri; 7-11pm Sat, Sun. **Average** €€. **Credit** MC, V.
One of the more authentic Moroccan restaurants in Brussels, Vie Sauvage is tucked away in a quiet residential street; you'll even have to ring a doorbell to gain entry. The owners have made an effort to transport their diners to the heat and dustiness of north Africa with the hanging pots and earthen walls, but it's the food that ultimately impresses the most. The full menu of specialities includes tagines and couscous, and there's also a wide range of salads. Service can be erratic and so the restaurant is probably to be avoided if you're in a

hurry. But if you're not, just relax, take in the mellow atmosphere and check out the lengthy and unlikely list of scotch whiskies.

Vini e Antipasti

28 rue du Berger (0477 26 14 87). Métro Porte de Namur. **Meals served** noon-6pm Mon-Wed; noon-3pm, 7.30pm-midnight Thur, Fri; 7.30pm-midnight Sat. **Average €€€. No credit cards**.

At first glance, the tiny black frontage of this Italian enoteca looks like it might belong to a wine merchant's: the right-hand wall is constructed of a soaring wine rack, and an aged oak barrel hangs from the ceiling. In fact, it's a characterful introduction to one of Brussels' tiniest restaurants. This is one of those places where off-duty chefs come to eat, as much for the buzz and laughter as for the olive oil-rich mains, exquisite Italian snacks and pasta dishes, and marvellous wild boar sausage. (Febrile imaginations also suspect secret lodge-like activities among the cuisiniers, with white Umbrian truffles changing hands in crumpled brown packages.) Booking is essential, as the place is the size of a broom cupboard.

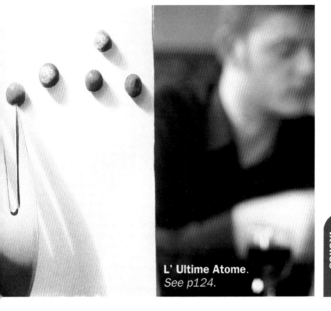

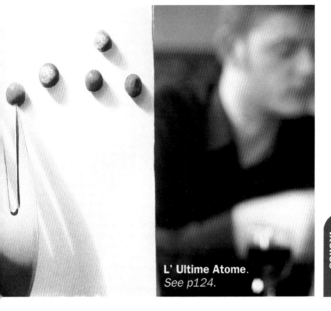

L' Ultime Atome.
See p124.

Ixelles

Bars

L'Amour Fou

185 chaussée d'Ixelles (02 514 27 09). Métro Porte de Namur/bus 54, 71. **Open** 11am-1am Mon-Thur, Sun; 11am-2am Fri, Sat. **Credit** AmEx, DC, MC, V.

An ever-popular arty bar-diner off place Fernand Cocq and on the other side of the road from the lovely Maison Communale, a grand house bought by violinist Bériot for his newly wedded lady, Spanish singer La Malibran. The kind of love going on opposite is of a lustier nature, as trendy twentysomethings canoodle between obligatory drags on their fags. The decor – strange chandeliers, shapeless art – and the gratuitous spread of fashion magazines would keep the solitary visitor occupied for a while, too, and the food really isn't bad. Dress reasonably smartly and you're bound to fit in, particularly if you're feeling flirtatious. In any case, if it doesn't appeal, there are plenty of other options around the square, particularly on early summer evenings when there are few better places to be in Brussels.

L'Atelier

77 rue Elise (02 649 19 53). Métro Louise/tram 93, 94/bus 71. **Open** 6pm-2.30am daily. **No credit cards**.
Forget the above-mentioned transport instructions and take a taxi: this place is worth both the effort and the expense. Tucked away amid drab streets 'twixt Ixelles' lakes and cemetery, L'Atelier is a little gem, an oasis for the discerning beer-drinker. A modest counter dividing the front of house and buzzing back area can barely hide the immodesty of a capacious fridge full of beers of almost every conceivable type, their names diligently felt-tipped in pink pen on the transparent doors. The draught choices aren't to be sniffed at, either, with Chouffe and Pecheresse among them. The beer buffs mingle with the intellectual end of the student fraternity from the nearby university.

Bar Parallèle

27 place Fernand Cocq (02 512 30 41). Métro Porte de Namur/bus 54, 71. **Open** 10am-1am Mon-Sat; 5pm-1am Sun. **No credit cards**.
One of a scattering of fashionable outlets whose terraces embellish this lively, uneven square, the Parallel Bar draws a younger, less fashion-conscious crowd than the lovelies who flock to L'Amour Fou nearby. A large, plain interior – this was until fairly recently a traditional old beer hall – fills with intellectual chatter from early evening, before a post-dinner influx keeps the place nicely ticking over until past midnight at weekends. A modest selection of meals and appetisers is served by a gratifyingly attentive wait-staff.

Café Belga

18 place Flagey (02 640 35 08). Bus 71. **Open** 9.30am-2am Mon-Thur, Sun; 9.30am-3am Fri, Sat. **No credit cards**.
The latest and most prestigious venue from the Nicolay group, the Belga occupies the ground floor and terrace of the equally swank Institut National de Radiodiffusion, a world-class 1930s broadcast hall painstakingly – and painfully – renovated after being boarded up in 1995. A similarly dilatory restoration process saw the INR tease classical music lovers with promises of various opening dates during the early 2000s; Nicolay and his men had the café stripped, its zinc bar and 1950s fittings soldered, the floor sanded for tiling and the wooden furniture sparklingly polished. And not a bad effort, either. The selection of drinks, pastries and sandwiches may not be adventurous – counter service is the norm – and the omnipresent scaffolding prevented the Belga from opening its terrace for summer in 2002, but it's still a worthy addition to the cultural life of the city.

For exotic groceries such as dried fish and green plantains, head to **African Asian Foods** (25 chaussée de Wavre). The smell of the spices will transport you to other worlds.

Do the Congo

In the early 1960s, waves of students came from Africa to Brussels to study, shortly after Congo gained its independence from Belgium, and began to gather in the streets near Porte de Namur.

However, these were not fleeting visits; at least, not all of them. Many students stuck around the area, which eventually came to be known as Matongé after a suburb in the Congolese capital of Kinshasa. Four decades on, the tangle of streets around chaussée de Wavre and chaussée d'Ixelles is home to a thriving African community of bars, restaurants, nightclubs and exotic food shops.

The heart of the Matongé is in the Galerie d'Ixelles, a shopping mall linking chaussée de Wavre with chaussée d'Ixelles. In line with the name of the neighbourhood, the two sides of the Galerie are named after streets in Kinshasa: Kanda-Kanda, packed with beauty salons, and the café-crammed Inzia. Stalls spill on to the streets here, and it's hard to differentiate one place from the next. However, don't miss the grocery shops, filled with spices from Madagascar and the Ivory Coast, exotic fruit, and even smoked insects (locust, anyone?).

At night, Matongé's main thoroughfare is the good-humoured rue de Longue Vie, pedestrianised and filled with bars and clubs. Restaurants such as **La Makossa** (18 rue de la Paix) turn out dishes made with chicken, curried lamb and even goat. At **l'Horloge de Sud** (*see p122*), meanwhile, you can accompany your beer with a traditional fish stew, sometimes made with specially imported dried fish.

That said, the whole of the Matongé is vibrant and alive, at weekends in particular, and you'll have no trouble finding fine food. Be warned, though: spices and peppers are used with reckless abandon, and it'll likely be hot stuff. Also in the area is an assortment of decent bars, plus some rather idiosyncratic dance bars, packed to the gills. Bear in mind it all has to close down by 2am, so get there early, take a deep breath and dive in.

A modern brasserie with the best from our past

Fine brasserie cuisine and local flavours
Grill and Rotisserie Specialities

Weekly Menu's @ 25 € per person
Weekly Business Lunches @ 12 € for two courses, including wine
Art Brunches on Sundays

Brasserie **S** Le sauvoir

Rue P. Devaux/P. Devauxstraat 1 | 1000 Brussels
T. 02 516 9100 | F. 02 516 9000 | www.lesauvoir.be

The delicatessen favoured by the rich of Ixelles, **Maison Félix** (14 rue Washington) sells luxury food and wine. It's pricey, but the Parisian ice-cream Berthillon is well worth the euros.

Le Châtelain

17 place du Châtelain (02 538 67 94). Métro Louise/ tram 81, 82, 91, 92. **Open** 10.30am-1.30am Mon-Fri. **Credit** AmEx, DC, MC, V.

This friendly, local bar-diner on a pretty square is surrounded by average Irish bars haunted by expats without the good grace to make the jump out to Tervuren. A small bar area, dominated by a huge Johnnie Walker sign, divides into a side room of bar tables and a back area facing a busy kitchen. Lunchtimes, particularly post-market Thursdays, are given over to unpretentious dishes of soups, steaks and salads, but in the evening, JW seems to tap his cane, and a livelier, younger crowd emerge to enjoy a diverting scene amid the old advertising posters and a soundtrack of mainstream jazz, blues and rock.

The Crow

520 avenue Louise (02 640 41 00). Métro Louise, then tram 23, 90, 93 or 94. **Open** 3pm-1.30am Mon-Thur; 3pm-3am Fri; 4pm-3am Sat. **Credit** AmEx, DC, MC, V.

Although of the same family as Fat Boy's over in the EU Quarter (*see p94*), and avidly expatriate to boot, the popular Crow has enough character to raise it from the mire of bog-standard Irish/Brit pubs on the eastern side of town. If anything, it's international; well, as international as karaoke and happy hour, anyway. The beer and cocktail lists are suitably diverse, the live music offerings of a Thursday or Friday engender a regular, friendly if unadventurous crowd happy to laugh along with it, and the bar staff tend to remember your name after a couple of visits. If you have to drink in Expatria, there are far worse places.

Le Grain d'Orge

142 chaussée de Wavre (02 511 26 47). Métro Porte de Namur. **Open** 11am-3am Mon-Sat; 6pm-3am Sun. **Credit** MC, V.

The guitar is still God here at the Grain, where its pot-bellied followers wallow in its Friday night malpractice (eg Fried Bourbon) surrounded by posters of past protagonists (eg The Who). On the six nights of the week when drinkers are not being assailed by barking four-piece combos, barmen with tattooed palms (doesn't that hurt?) serve a range of beers in this spit-and-more-spit saloon to an audience of ponytails and roll-up smokers. Some bring forgiving ladyfriends. After they argue – and they will, in all likelihood – you'll find the men propped up in the Tulipe diagonally opposite, a mosaic-tiled retreat for unshaven losers extracting cheer and excuses from 75¢ beer.

Ixelles

L'Horloge du Sud

*141 rue du Trône (02 512 18 64). Métro Trône/bus 95,
96.* **Open** noon-midnight Mon-Fri; 5pm-1am Sat, Sun.
Credit AmEx, MC, V.

An easy introduction to the African quarter of Brussels,
l'Horloge is located on the main drag fronting a hotchpotch of streets housing a plethora of lively and
occasionally lurid African bars, rue Longue Vie in
particular. What l'Horloge loses in immediacy, it more
than makes up for in space and comfort. There's no bar
crush here, but a loose collection of old tables and chairs,

Season's eatings

As it has in most countries in
the west, truly seasonal food
in Belgium has become a
thing of the past. Fresh daily
deliveries flown in from around
the world, while undoubtedly
being of benefit to the
adventurous consumer,
have rather put paid to such
foodstuffs' exoticism. But
there are still some seasonal
traditions peculiar to Belgium
that come round each year as
surely as a strawberry in June.

The tradition that infiltrates
most into the Belgian psyche is
la chasse, or the hunt. Come
November and December each
year, it's game season. Most
of the game sold here is local:
not to Brussels itself, though
the Fôret de Soignes used to
be choice hunting ground in
the good old days, but to the
Ardennes, the richly forested
area that rolls down towards
Luxembourg. From here comes
venison, boar, wild rabbit, hare
and a clutch of birds, including
pigeon and pheasant.

Game is usually roasted, but
the less tender cuts are used
in casseroles with deep red

wine sauces, often enriched
with a touch of Belgian
chocolate. Most typically
Belgian restaurants will include
game on their menus around
this time, with some places
even running a whole game
special. In Brussels, a good
place for game is the **Roue
d'Or** (*see p30*); if in Antwerp,
try **Adriaan** (*see p165*).

While asparagus is around
all year, the true Belgian stuff
pushes through in May. Locals
prefer the great fat white
variety, and once the season
rolls around, it becomes a
cheap, everyday item, albeit
only for a few weeks. The
Flemish cook asparagus à
la flamande, with butter,
chopped egg and sometimes
breadcrumbs; it's a dish
favoured by many restaurants.

Another typical and popular
vegetable at this time of year
are young houblons: hop
shoots, rustled up with cream
and nutmeg or poached in
soups and casseroles. Unlike
asparagus, the hop generally
doesn't make it on to the
tables of Brussels restaurants

plants, warrior statues, musical instruments and a massive mirror, all of which merge woozily as the drum rhythms and plentiful selection of Caribbean rums kick in. There's African and Belgian cuisine, and live music.

Le Pantin

355 chaussée d'Ixelles (02 640 80 91). Bus 71. **Open** 11am-2am Mon-Sat; 2pm-2am Sun. **No credit cards**.
Before the area on the other side of Ixelles Ponds by the university became swamped with trendy bars, Le Pantin was a classic spot for students of the old school raised

at any other time of year. You can try them at **La Grande Porte** (*see p137*).

As summer moves in, the usual range of soft fruits floods the markets. And as long as local farmers resist the temptation to pick them too early, Belgian strawberries are usually of a decent quality. The strawberry strain found here is a little more blousy than its English counterpart; some are so big they need slicing. But the sweetness and softness are definitely there.

Summer is also the time for fresh herring from the North Sea, a tradition that has spread down to Brussels from the Netherlands and Flanders. If you're feeling squeamish, it's worth remembering that they are eaten raw, preferably

between thumb and forefinger with head thrown back. If you don't want to end up doing a bad pelican impersonation, they look quite presentable on plates throughout Ste-Catherine, or in traditional restaurants such as **Aux Armes de Bruxelles** (*see p33*).

If you're keen on coming to Belgium for the mussels, then be warned: though the season generally runs from late August/early September through to April, it's a slightly moveable feast. It's all to do with breeding times and the desire of allowing the mussels to grow to the required size. It's taken seriously, too: in 2002, an official edict delayed the opening of the season because it was judged that the black-shelled ones were not yet plump enough. While you can find mussels from other parts of the world in supermarkets all year round, Belgian restaurants will not substitute. You'll only be able to mussel in at restaurants here during the season, after which time the black pots will be scrubbed up and put away for a few months.

Ixelles

on chess, cheap cigarettes and esoteric conversation. Beatniks would be too kind a description, but you get the picture. Keeping these junior philosophers in check and suitable discomfort were creaky wooden furniture and goateed bar staff, surrounded by a quirky collection of toys, games and old posters. While the Pantin remains the same, many of its potential customers have moved on, and little short of a major sea change in music and decor will woo them back. A much loved bar, nonetheless.

Rick's

334 avenue Louise (02 647 75 30). Métro Louise, then tram 93, 94. **Open** 11am-midnight Mon-Sat. **Credit** AmEx, DC, MC, V.

As the original play said, everybody comes to Rick's. OK, everyone in a linen jacket and tie comes to Rick's, the most established – and still the most stylish – American bar in town. Much like Rick's place in *Casablanca*, this recently renovated establishment is swish, chic and pricey, in this case housed in a magnificent three-storey edifice on elegant avenue Louise. In summer, the rear terrace comes into its own, and all that seems to be missing is a roulette wheel and a crazy Russian barman.

Le Stoemelings

7 place de Londres (02 512 43 74). Métro Trône. **Open** 11am-2am Mon-Fri; 5pm-2am Sat, Sun. **No credit cards**.

A cosy cubby-hole of a bar, tucked away in a little square between the ring road and the hubbub of African Ixelles. The lived-in wooden interior takes in an intimate scattering of tables, two prime window seats and a tall bar counter ideal for propping up. Hearty Belgian fodder complements a laudable range of local beers, mainly bottled. Regulars – sprightly alcoholics, old grunters with axes too rusty to grind, bearded intellectuals in bad jumpers – are joined by students who'll look back on the friendly, carefree Stoemelings as epitomising their salad days. Nice bar staff, too.

L'Ultime Atome

14 rue St-Boniface (02 511 13 67). Métro Porte de Namur. **Open** 9am-midnight Mon-Thur; 9am-12.30am Fri, Sat. **Credit** MC, V.

This vast, fashionable corner bar-resto has been essential to the trendification of this enclave in the shadow of St-Boniface church. Business begins early here, a busy breakfast trade merging into slow brunch and a clock-watching lunchtime crowd; the kitchen is open all day, and the effervescent waiters never seem to stop. By the evening, tables are scarce and talk is incessant, a mixed, fashionable clientele somehow making themselves understood over the boom of bog-standard electronic boogie. The beer list could run to a small book – 50 at least – and the food is acceptable Fulham International.

St-Gilles

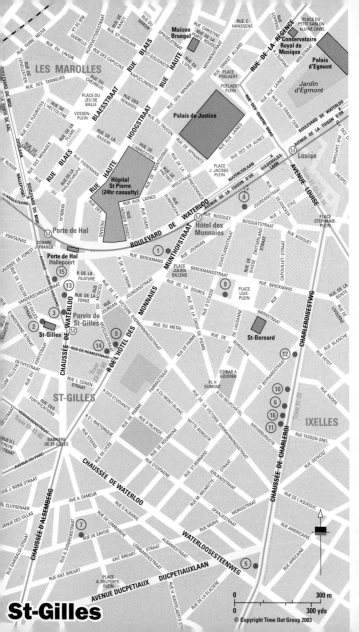

RUE C HANSSENS
PLACE DU PETIT SABLON
KLEINE ZAVEL

Maison Bruegel
Conservatoire Royal de Musique
Palais d'Egmont

RUE C
RUE CHRISTINE
RUE DE LA
PORTE ROUGE
RUE DE
EFFE

SPIEGELSTRAAT
RUE ST-GHISLAIN
RUE DES CAPUCINS
CAPUCIJNENSTR

RUE TERRE-NEUVE
QUERELLE
RUE DE NANCY
RUE DU MIROIR

RUE DES CORDIERS
BEG
CORDIERSTR
RUE DE LA RÉGENCE

Jardin d'Egmont

RUE ERNEST ALLARD
RUE DUPONT

PLACE POELAERT

RUE DU LAVOIR
BOULEVARD DU MIDI
RUE DE LENGLENTIER
RUE DES TANNEURS
RUE DU CHEVREUIL

PLACE DU JEU DE BALLE
VOSSEN-PLEIN

LES MAROLLES
RUE BLAES
RUE HAUTE
HOOGSTRAAT
BLAESSTRAAT

RUE DES MINIMES
RUE DES RENARDS
RUE DES MINIMES

Palais de Justice

RUE AUX LAINES
RUE DES QUATRE BRAS

Louise
M
AVENUE DE LA TOISON D'OR
BOULEVARD DE WATERLOO

RUE DE LA
RASIERE
RUE DE LA
PHILANTHROPIE
RUE PIERMANS
RUE DE
L'ABRICOTIER

Hôpital St Pierre
(24hr casualty)

RUE AUX LAINES
RUE DE WYNANTS
PLACE J JACOBS-PLEIN
WATERLOOLAAN
RUE DES SIX AUNES
GUIDELINES LAAN

M Porte de Hal
Square F Franck
Porte de Hal Halleport
FONTAINAS
CHAUSSÉE DE FOREST

BOULEVARD DE WATERLOO
RUE BERGER BORDET
RUE DES PAVONS

Hôtel des Monnaies

AVENUE LOUISE

15
13
3
St-Gilles
Parvis de St-Gilles

R DE LA FILATURE
R DE LA FORGE
RUE DE MOSCOU
RUE JOURDAN
RUE DE LA VICTOIRE
OVERWINNINGSSTRAAT

RUE BERCKMANS
PLACE JULIEN DILLENS
RUE DE LA SOURCE
RUE DE LA CROIX DE PIERRE

1
Hôtel des Monnaies
RUE JOURDAN
RUE BOSQUET
JOURDANSTRAAT
BOSQUETSTRAAT
RUE BOSQUET

8
PLACE LOIX-PLEIN
RUE D'ÉCOSSE
RUE DE LAUSANNE
BRONSTRAAT

RUE DE SUISSE
ZWITSERLAND-STRAAT
CAPOUILLET-STRAAT
RUE BERCKMANS

PLACE STÉPHANIE-PLEIN

9
14
St-Bernard

CHAUSSÉE DE WATERLOO
R DU HÔTEL DES MONNAIES
CHAUSSÉE DE ROMESTRAAT

RUE DU METAL
RUE DE PARME
RUE DE PIERRE
RUE DE BORDEAUX

12
10
6
16
11
IXELLES

CHARLEROI ESTWG
RUE VEYDT
RUE BLANCHE
RUE DE LA BONTE
RUE FADER

ST-GILLES
DETHYSTRAAT
RUE DES FORTIFICATIONS
VERMEULENSTRAAT
BARRIÈRE DE ST-GILLES

R DES ÉTUDIANTS
R D L RHETORIQUE
RUE STEENS
RUE DE PARME
R DU MONT-BLANC
R D'IRLANDE
RUE DE ROUMANIE
RUE ST-BERNARD
WITTE BERNSTR
PLH DUMONT
SQ BAR A BOUVIER
RUE DU NEUCHÂTEL
RUE DE LA VICTOIRE
OVERWINNINGSSTRAAT
RUE NEUWBURGSTR

Train 91-92
CHAUSSÉE DE CHARLEROI
RUE TASSON-SNEL
RUE DEFACQZ

7
CHAUSSÉE DE WATERLOO
AVE A DEMEUR
RUE D'ALBANIE
RUE DE LOMBARDIE
RUE DE SAVOIE
Train 16 & 92
RUE J ROBIE STRAAT
A CLUYSENAER
VENUE DES VILLAS
RUE GARIBALDI STRAAT

RUE M WILMOTTE
RUE MORRISSTRAAT
IERLANDSTRAAT
RUE ESPAGNE
RUE ST-BERNARD
SPANJESTRAAT
RUE DE L'AQUEDUC
RUE AMÉRICAINE

N
WATERLOOSESTEENWEG
5
ANT BREART
PLACE A DELPORTE-PLEIN
ALBANIESTRAAT
LOMBARDIESTRAAT
RUE AFRICAINE

AVENUE DUCPETIAUX
DUCPETIAUXLAAN
R W NAPELAERTS ST
RUE DE LA GLACIÈRE

0   300 m
0   300 yds

St-Gilles

© Copyright Time Out Group 2003

More than most areas of Brussels, St-Gilles is a community of contrasts. Here you will find working-class Bruxellois, large populations of north African and Spanish residents and some of the grandest art nouveau houses in the city. Along the chaussée de Charleroi is a run of grand restaurants in converted townhouses; over by parvis de St-Gilles is a clutch of good-quality Moroccan places; and at the bottom end of chaussée de Waterloo is a Spanish enclave. Threaded through all these cultural pockets is a collection of local Belgian bars, and other restaurants of every nationality and price range. Up and coming but not quite there yet, St-Gilles is ripe for exploration and discovery.

St-Gilles

Restaurants

Belgian & French

Caviar House (10a rue Jean Stas) stocks caviar, vodka, foie gras and a specialist selection of French vintages. It's a top-notch deli, but at top-notch prices.

Les Capucines ★

22 rue Jourdan (02 538 69 24). Métro Louise. **Meals served** noon-3pm, 6-11.30pm daily. **Average** €€€.
Credit AmEx, DC, MC, V.

One of St-Gilles's finer restaurants, Capucines is located towards the smart-hotel end of the petit ring, where the grand old houses edge towards the rather more modern motorway. But step inside and you'll immediately be becalmed by a sophisticated Philippe Starck interior. Chef Pierre Burtomboy, who trained with famed superstar chef Jean-Pierre Bruneau, offers fine French dining with a Belgian edge, which entails less pretension and more on the plate: langoustines with morels braised in vin jaune, say, or turbot with caramelised endive and a beurre-blanc. The clientele tend to be wealthy, though the set menus (€17 lunch, €25-€52 dinner) are good value.

Chelsea Wine Bar

85 chaussée de Charleroi (02 544 19 77). Tram 91, 92.
Meals served noon-2.30pm, 7pm-midnight daily.
Average €€€. **Credit** AmEx, DC, MC, V.

The entrance to the small, intimate Chelsea is less St-Gilles and more Park Lane, marble stairs leading up to a room with saffron-coloured walls, Greek(-ish) columns and dark teak furniture. The atmosphere's soothing, in a gentlemen's club kind of way; there's even a cigar bar at the back, stocked with choice Cubans. The food matches the feel: classic French, with particularly notable foie gras, escargots and wild salmon. Chelsea is also proud of its wines: the menu runs to around 40, from New Worlds through to French vintages. Dress up a little if you don't want to feel out of place, but be confident that a meal here isn't at all a daunting experience.

Inada ★

73 rue de la Source (02 538 01 13). Métro Hôtel des Monnaies. **Meals served** noon-2.30pm, 7-10pm Tue-Fri; 7-10pm Sat. **Average** €€€€. **Credit** MC, V.

If and when all the mussels wear you down and you can take no more Belgian, head here. The restaurant, named after and run by chef Saburo Inada, aims to blend the French with the Japanese. Such a collision of influences

St-Gilles

The best Nouveau-deco

Aux Armes de Bruxelles
Chip in. *See p33.*

Les Brasseries Georges
We'll always have Paris. *See p147.*

Comme Chez Soi
Opulence under the stars. *See p27.*

Falstaff
Great shakes. *See p37.*

La Porteuse d'Eau
Drink it in. *See p134.*

De Ultieme Hallucinatie
See it and believe it. *See p151.*

is noticeable not just in the decor – the dining room's low-key, though each white linen-clad table comes with its own little individual Zen pebble garden – but also in the food. Typical dishes? Caramelised pigeon in a sweet and sour sauce, a French classic decidedly enlivened with Asian spices and flavourings. Inada also has a reputation for its wines, and you'd do well to allow the staff to match the wine with the food. Expensive, but worth the treat.

Le Kolya ★

106 chaussée de Charleroi (02 533 18 30). Tram 91, 92. **Meals served** noon-2.30pm, 6-11pm Mon-Fri; 6pm-midnight Sat. **Average** €€€. **Credit** AmEx, DC, MC, V.

A stylish place, this, perfect for either a discreet business meeting or a first-date liaison. La Kolya has two very distinct atmospheres: a plush red dining room, complete with animal skins on the walls, and a little less formal glass conservatory and umbrella'd terrace. The menu is French, with a big nod to the south: mullet with lemon and olives, carpaccio of beef with fresh truffles, grilled prawns with papaya and mint. It ain't cheap, but the fine set menu at lunchtimes (€15) is a lot less wallet-ruining than the evening carte. La Kolya is part of the splendid Manos hotel chain, but has its own street entrance.

Le Living Room

50 chaussée de Charleroi (02 534 44 34). Tram 91, 92. **Meals served** 7pm-midnight Mon-Sat. **Average** €€€. **Credit** AmEx, MC, V.

The Living Room has become a well-loved institution among the trendy and well-heeled of St-Gilles: a mix and match of New York diner and Paris lounge bar, it serves mostly Asian food (sushi, sashimi and Thai dishes). The decor is a bit overwhelming, but constant encouragement from flouncy TV interior designers means that diners accept (almost) anything these days. Low-slung seats will help you relax while tucking into the large portions of high-calibre food. It's a great place to come with a group of pals, as there's no need to keep your voices down. As with most of Belgium, you can opt for a non-smoking or secondary-smoking space.

Ma Folle de Soeur

53 chaussée de Charleroi (02 538 22 39). Métro Louise/ tram 91, 92. **Meals served** noon-2.15pm, 7-10.30pm Mon-Fri. **Average** €€. **Credit** AmEx, DC, MC, V.

Run by two sisters (the name roughly translates as 'my mad sister'), this small restaurant sells itself so well from the street outside that you'd be hard-pushed to walk by it without being tempted to stop in for a bite. A long bar dominates, but the overall effect is softened at night by the sun-yellow walls and soft candlelight. The menu,

The atmospheric street market at **parvis de St-Gilles** is open 6am-12.30pm Tue-Sun, offering fruit, veg, cheese, bread and a selection of north African goodies.

St-Gilles

Aux Mille
et Une Nuits. See p132.

Belgian in nature with French bistro influences, has flair; the meat (duck, steak, even horse fillet) comes dressed in imaginative sauces, but there's usually some fish swimming around on the menu, too. Businessfolk in suits give way to young lovers and pals in the evening.

Salons de l'Atalaïde ★

89 chaussée de Charleroi (02 537 21 54). Tram 91, 92.
Meals served noon-3pm. 7-11.30pm daily. **Average**
€€€. **Credit** AmEx, MC, V.

Ornate chandeliers, oversized paintings, Gothic candles and ostentatious palms combine to give Salons de l'Atalaïde, a former auction house, a surreal edge. To your left as you enter is a small window table and sofas, perfect for afternoon tea. But once you step through to the main room, you'll be astonished at the size of the place. The bistro-style menu is big on choice – gamekeeper's hare rubs shoulders with scampi sushi, Irish rib steak with fish lasagne – but do save room for the tarte au sucre for dessert. Yep, they really do mean sugar tart. And it's absolutely to die for. You'll need to book in advance, as this is one of the town's most popular restaurants.

Rue Jourdan
and **rue
Jean Stas**,
pedestrian-
ised streets
at the top end
of avenue
Louise,
are full of
restaurants,
from pizzerias
to fine French
operations.
It's full of
atmosphere in
the summer
when the
terraces open.

International

Araucana

*63 rue de l'Hôtel des Monnaies (02 539 25 76). Métro
Hôtel des Monnaies.* **Meals served** 7pm-midnight
Tue-Sun. **Average** €€. **Credit** MC, V.

This little cantina doesn't specialise in the food of any
one country in particular, instead offering dishes that are
more generically south American. The emphasis is on
Mexican – the guacamole and the chilli con carne both
hit the spot – but travel south down the menu and you'll
find spicy chicken- and chick pea-infused offerings from
Chile (plus some very decent Chilean wines). Latin
American musicians strum away throughout, and the
open kitchen adds to the bustling feel. Kids are welcome;
there's even a special children's menu, a little lighter on
the spices. Araucana is used by locals of all nationalities,
though in recent months, non-St-Gilleans have started to
discover it.

Casablanca

277 chaussée de Charleroi (02 544 09 68). Tram 91, 92.
Meals served noon-2.30pm, 6.30-11pm Mon, Wed-Sun.
Average €. **Credit** MC, V.

The feature that, above all others, marks Casablanca out
from other north African restaurants in Brussels is its log
fire. In winter, it's used to keep the punters warm, but it's
also operational year-round as an oven. The smell of
dripping lamb will hit you as soon as you walk into this
traditional, informal eatery, and will then be served up to
you in a wonderfully heady mix of prunes, cinnamon and
sesame. The similarly grilled pigeon breasts are also a
treat. Friday and Saturday nights are party nights: belly-
dancing action!

Le Jugurtha

*34 rue du Moscou (02 538 23 67). Pré-métro Parvis de
St-Gilles.* **Meals served** noon-2.30pm, 6-11pm Mon-Wed,
Fri-Sun; 6-11pm Thur. **Average** €€. **Credit** AmEx,
MC, V.

Madame Fabienne arrived in St-Gilles 25 years ago and
still inhabits the same area along with her little restaurant
Jugurtha. French-Algerian by birth, she decided to style
the restaurant's food along the length of the Maghreb,
incorporating Moroccan and Tunisian food onto her
menu. To be honest, the restaurant looks a bit tacky, but
the menu is great value, and includes the usual run of
tagines, couscous and brik, a type of deep-fried croquette
made from thin pastry and stuffed with tuna or egg and
olives. Even the wines are drawn from these corners of
the world. Nothing outstanding, sure; just an honest,
friendly neighbourhood restaurant.

St-Gilles

El Madrileño

50 chaussée de Waterloo (02 537 69 82). Pré-métro Parvis de St-Gilles. **Meals served** noon-3pm, 6-11pm Mon, Tue, Fri-Sun; noon-3pm Wed. **Average** €€. **No credit cards.**

At the bottom end of the chaussée, extending round to the Gare du Midi, is a Spanish community that has made its mark on the area with an assortment of restaurants, bars and shops. This family-run place has a strong Spanish clientele, who mostly gather in the back room. Who knows what they're up to, but they're probably just making the most of the mighty paella and milk-fed pork served up by old Andrino. Over the bar hang great legs of serrano ham; in little trays on top of it are sardines in oil, plump olives and spicy little meatballs. You'd need to go to Spain to get anything nearly as authentic.

Aux Mille et Une Nuits ★

7 rue du Moscou (02 537 41 27/www.au-mille-et-une-nuits.be). Pré-métro Parvis de St-Gilles. **Meals served** noon-3pm, 6-11.30pm Mon-Sat. **Average** €€€. **Credit** AmEx, DC, MC, V.

This Tunisian restaurant, which sits among a cluster of north African eateries, is an over-the-top place. Rugs and camel bags festoon the walls, while above, hundreds of tiny lights twinkle down on diners, a make-believe desert sky. Once you've taken all this in, take a look at the menu. Traditional tagines and couscous are the order of the day, but then there's also caramelised shank of lamb and honeyed chicken in pastry. Whatever you have, it'll likely be out of this world, and served with style.

Bars

Brasserie de l'Union

55 parvis de St-Gilles (02 538 15 79). Pré-métro Parvis de St-Gilles. **Open** 8am-1am daily. **No credit cards.**

A bohemian bar happy to serve the local community at large – some befriended solely by spaniels, deep in one-way conversations – the Union comprises a large room whose picture windows are fringed with touches of blue and yellow. On alternate weekends, coaches leave here for obscure swathes of Wallonia, bearing a cheery throng of local supporters ('Allez l'Union!'). A Sunday morning's market browsing is bookended by an accordionist squeezing out tunes incapable of drowning out the din of children running amok. After they depart, along with the spaniels, the squeezeboxers and the senile, the night is given over to a chain-smoking gang of Bukowksi-esque thirst. Not pretty, but somehow compulsive.

Champignac (108 chaussée d'Alsemberg) is a wild mushroom emporium, selling not only the musty fungi, but everything you need to prepare them (including recipes).

Brasserie Verscheuren.
See p134.

Brasserie Verscheuren

*11-13 parvis de St-Gilles (02 539 40 68). Pré-métro
Parvis de St-Gilles.* **Open** 11am-1am Mon; 8am-2am
Tue-Sun. **No credit cards**.

The classier of the corner bars serving the parvis, the
Verscheuren twinkles with art deco touches. Three rows
of tables and banquettes are waited on by an erratic staff
safe in the knowledge that few of the boho-intellectual
regulars pay much attention as to why they came here in
the first place; the Verscheuren is simply their natural
habitat, drink or no drink. If they cared to look up, they'd
find a more than adequate selection of beers – including
bottled rarities such as Pecheresse – complemented by a
hearty lunch menu. Almost incongruous with the classic
station clock and delicate window panelling, a vast league
ladder of football club names from the lower local
divisions occupies the back wall.

Chez Moeder Lambic

*68 rue de Savoie (02 539 14 19). Pré-métro Horta/
tram 18, 81, 82.* **Open** 4-9pm Mon; 4pm-3am Tue-Sun.
No credit cards.

Happy to collect dust behind St-Gilles' town hall, the
collectors' cavern of Chez Moeder Lambic hides from the
outside world behind beer-labelled windows. Inside it's a
dark hive, three long shelves of obscure bottles framing
the bar counter and wooden tables of differing cuts. For
those who have sampled every cobwebbed example, racks
of comic books line the wall under the window. Outsiders
can only guesstimate the number of brews, daring to stab
at four figures. Insiders? If they know, they're not letting
on, but they've probably recorded it by quill in the
weighty tome under the counter, another collector's item
collecting dust while the outside world and his wife guzzle
mass-produced lagers in brighter bars.

La Porteuse d'Eau

*48 avenue Jean Volders (02 537 66 46). Pré-métro Parvis
de St-Gilles.* **Open** 10am-midnight daily. **Credit** MC, V.

A genteel café done out in an ornate art nouveau style,
its character quickly announced by delicate portraits of
water carriers outside and a grand front door ushering
you into a houseplant-ridden interior. Almost hidden by
greenery, a spiral staircase leads to an atrium themed
with friezes of more water women, overlooking a
scattering of intimate tables. Lemon tea and fine pastries
are the order of the day, although the usual range of beers
is on offer, along with pastas for those with a less-than-
genteel hunger. Located on a grey road linking St-Gilles
with the urban grime surrounding Midi Station, La
Porteuse would clean up in a more refined area. Here, it
sticks out like a carefully manicured thumb.

**Mig's World
Wines** (43
chaussée
de Charleroi)
specialises
in New World
wines in
a classy
designer
shop. Pop by
for a tasting
and some
sound advice
from Mig
himself on
Saturdays.

Les Marolles

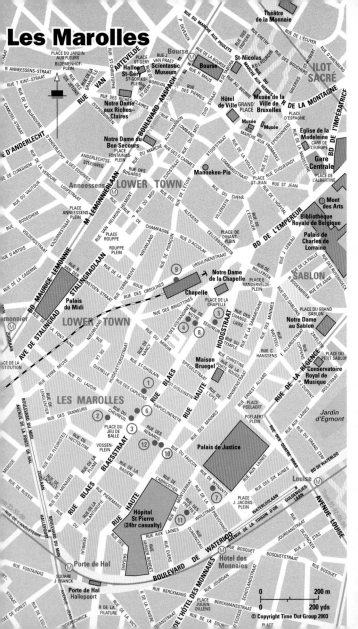

MAP KEY

1. Bazaar *p139*
2. Chez Marcel *p142*
3. La Clef d'Or *p143*
4. La Grande Porte *p137*
5. L'Idiot du Village *p138*
6. Indigo *p144*
7. Les Larmes du Tigre *p140*
8. Les Petits Oignons *p139*
9. Recyclart *p144*
10. Le Renard *p144*
11. Au Stekerlaplatte *p139*
12. Het Warm Water *p141*

Les Marolles was originally a stridently working-class area. The network of tiny streets bisected by rue Blaes and rue Haute still remains, and its once socialist heart now lies in the daily flea market on place du Jeu de Balle. Around this square are cafés and bars that reflect the area's personality: resolutely Bruxellois while still cocking a snook at authority. Most of the restaurants in the area aim to attract a more refined clientele, representing not just a spillover from Sablon but also a certain residential gentrification. Yet Les Marolles still remains Brussels' most endearing and characterful *quartier*.

Restaurants

Belgian & French

La Grande Porte

9 rue Notre-Seigneur (02 512 89 98). Bus 20, 48.
Meals served noon-3pm, 6pm-2am Mon-Sat.
Average €€. **Credit** MC, V.
Beyond La Grande Porte's *grande porte* – a huge, studded, wooden thing – is a cosy room reminiscent of a Dutch brown café, with an old bar running along one wall. Turn a corner, though, and you could be in a different world. It seems as if this restaurant has been stitched together from two different patterns, the modern addition being rather soulless compared to the buzz of the flea-market main room. Wherever you sit, though, La Grande Porte is great for late-night eats. All the Belgian classics are here – mussels, steak with sauce, stoemp, waterzooi, deep bowls of fresh frites – and the extended hours attract artists, actors, musicians and groups of chums who don't want to go home just yet.

Les Marolles

La Grande Porte. *See p137.*

L'Idiot du Village

19 rue Notre-Seigneur (02 502 55 82). Bus 20, 48.
Meals served noon-2pm, 7.15-11pm Mon-Fri.
Average €€€. Credit AmEx, DC, MC, V.
This small bistro, much beloved by celebs, is hidden away in
a side street off the antiques-shopping thoroughfare of rue
Blaes. The chairs and tables are of the type you'd hope to find
in the nearby Jeu du Balle flea market, the walls midnight blue
and carmine, the flowers dried and the chandeliers kitsch. It
sounds faintly clichéd, yet it works perfectly, as does the
eclectic food served up by chef Alain Gascoin. It's decidedly
down-to-earth fare but extremely well-executed: expect dishes
along the lines of succulent rabbit and leek stew, full of wine
and herbs and totally heartening. Booking is essential.

The cafés around the flea market on **place du Jeu de Balle** are full of life in the mornings, especially on Sundays when there's music and a carnival atmosphere.

Les Petits Oignons

13 rue Notre-Seigneur (02 512 47 38). Bus 20, 48.
Meals served noon-2.30pm, 7-11pm Mon-Sat.
Average €€€. **Credit** AmEx, DC, MC, V.
From the outside, this fine, vine-covered house, which dates from the 17th century, looks as if it could have starred in a Breughel painting. Walking in, you'll feel welcomed and warmed, in winter by a blazing log fire, and in the summer on the green and lantern-lit terrace at the back. The food is unfussy French/Belgian fare, but it's cooked with finesse and arrives in invigorating portions; a veal cutlet resembles the size of a side of a horse, a fillet of dorade is thick and fleshy. Depending on the menu, staff may ask you to order desserts at the beginning of the meal. Difficult for purists, sure, but it only goes to show that this is a restaurant that likes to get the food absolutely right.

Au Stekerlaplatte

4 rue des Prêtres (02 512 86 81). Métro Hôtel des Monnaies. **Meals served** 7pm-1am Tue-Sun.
Average €€€. **Credit** MC, V.
At first glance, you may think Au Stekerlaplatte is full and turn to leave, but don't give up: this place is a real warren of rooms and corridors, and you should enter safe in the knowledge that there's bound to be a table somewhere. It's a friendly place, this, belying its rather offbeat (albeit slowly up-and-coming) location. The basic Belgian food is prepared in time-honoured fashion – the emphasis is on steaks and sauces served with great fat fries – but you might also find the likes of grilled pig's trotter, spare ribs and black pudding on the decidedly vegetarian-unfriendly menu. Whatever you choose, you'll be eating it among a growing number of people who pack into here after a trip to the cinema or the theatre, or crowds of young clubbers who are only just starting their evening at midnight.

International

Bazaar

63 rue des Capucins (02 511 26 00). Bus 20, 48.
Meals served 7.30-11pm Tue-Thur; 7.30-11.30pm Fri, Sat. **Average** €€€. **Credit** DC, MC, V.
For Bazaar, read bizarre. The decor at this restaurant is wilfully eccentric: rich drapes, low-slung Moroccan-style sofas, the junk-shop trinketry… and a huge hot air balloon suspended from the ceiling. The candlelight that illuminates the place is a nod back to its past as a convent, although its reported propensity for catching fire back in those days has – touch wood – not carried through to the 21st century. Certainly, the nuns would have a ball here

Les Marolles

Inside the Belgian bar

Beer tourism is all well and good, particularly in a city centre gleaming with gems. Bars unchanged since anno 1699, bars of heavyweight artistic heritage, bars with beers in 500 fruit flavours: all are worthy of your custom. But what of the humble local? The scores of everyday bars, among them **Chez Marcel** (*see p142*), **La Clef d'Or** (*see p143*) and **Le Renard** (*see p144*): their praises elsewhere unsung, what happens there in the mysterious haze of neon and Belga smoke?

The Belgian bar differs in character from its French, Dutch or German counterparts. 'The Dutch complain that crossing the border into Belgium marks the start of lawlessness. We Belgians claim that crossing the border into Holland marks the end of imagination,' is how one native put it (in a bar, funnily enough). Holland, built on uniformity, houses uniform bars. Going Dutch sees sensible people drinking sensibly. Provincial France can be just as stiflingly bland. Germany's bars can be varied, but rare is that twinkle of irony that keeps you coming back for more. In Belgium, this hotchpotch country that few – natives especially – can take seriously, the corner bar is where the sublime meets the ridiculous over drinks.

And these drinks will be unusual. Strawberry, sky blue or pink, served in its own logoed glass on to its own logoed beermat. Similarly, the bar interior will entice curiosity. Smoky, brown and unknowingly retro, this haven for the wantonly irregular may also boast the erratic neon of Belgian pinball, actually a fiendishly complicated local

now: world music floats through the ample space, with the downstairs cellar hosting disco and Latin nights at weekends. The food is adequate if eclectic, with north African dishes, Italian staples and unusual items such as carpaccio of ostrich. But people come here less for the nosh and more for the accompanying entertainment.

Les Larmes du Tigre

21 rue de Wynants (02 512 18 77). Métro Hôtel des Monnaies. **Meals served** noon-2.30pm, 7-10.30pm Mon, Wed-Fri; 7-10.30pm Sat; noon-3pm, 7-10pm Sun. **Average** €€. **Credit** AmEx, DC, MC, V.
Run by Marc Breukers and his sister Muriel, Les Larmes du Tigre is one of the best Thai restaurants in the city. The rigid townhouse in which it's set, in the shadow of the massive Palais de Justice, seems fresh and innocent, unlike many of its more temporary neighbours opposite. Inside, though, it's a riot of clean colour, white walls with

bingo betting game in pinball table form. In the other corner of the room, a unisex toilet will be guarded by a grumpy crone demanding a token sum for its use. Meet Madame Pipi.

Behind the bar, not only 57 varieties of beer, but a basket of boiled eggs, a box of Royco cup-a-soups and the promise of salami nibbles and cheese chunks on sticks, laid out for sharing on a wooden board. In a prominent position by the rules of the house, a photo of a dearly loved, long-lost pet, invariably an Alsatian. (A strange honour, given its lifetime of bored servitude imprisoned under a bar stool while master drank away entire winters.)

And what of conversation, wit, repartee? How many times, footloose, have you slipped dreamily from third to fourth beer fearfully anchored in ditchwater dull talk of do-it-yourself scheming, local house prices and dwindling interest rates? Not here. For Belgians are collectors. While their unchanging corner bars collect dust, the regulars collect football cards, vinyl, beermats.

Note, too, that Belgians are endearingly Anglophilic. Clock that Oxo box c1914 behind the bar, for a start, but mention a rare 45 on Parlophone, that Wolves full-back from the 1971-72 season or an obscure beer from Staffordshire, and don't expect to be leaving the bar much before midnight. Where else, in this standardised, homogenised, globalised Europe, is the obscure and the quirky celebrated so cheerily... and celebrated with such spectacular, spangle-coloured beers?

a swathe of multi-coloured parasols hanging from the ceiling, and a neat little walled terrace and conservatory that packs 'em in each summer. The food, meanwhile, is sublime; try the giant prawns in red curry sauce or the chicken in lemongrass and garlic with green chilli paste. On Sundays, there's a running buffet that includes starter and main course selections from the regular menu. Service is frighteningly efficient, even a little off-handish, but it doesn't stop crowds of professionals using it for business lunches or for dinner after a long day at the bar.

Het Warm Water

25 rue des Renards (02 513 91 59). Métro Porte de Hal/bus 20, 48. **Meals served** 8am-7pm Mon, Tue, Sun; 8am-9pm Thur-Sat. **Average** €. **No credit cards**.
Het Warm Water is a bit of a walk up a steepish hill from the flea market, but there are plenty of little shops at which you can stop on the way. It's an all-day breakfast

Les Larmes du Tigre. *See p140.*

Les Marolles

sort of place, serving eggs and waffles and toasts or more substantial baguettes and salads. There are meat dishes on the menu, but in this deeply carnivorous country, the extensive menu at Het Warm Water means it qualifies as one of Brussels' better vegetarian options. It's invariably busy, especially at weekends, but pop in and say you'll be back in half an hour and they'll keep you a table. It's popular with shoppers and traders alike, giving it a neighbourhood feel. Indeed, it's very much in keeping with the area: informal, busy, buzzy and great to flop in a while after all that junk-riffling at the bottom of the hill.

Bars

Chez Marcel
20 place du Jeu de Balle (02 511 13 75). Bus 20, 48.
Open 8am-4pm daily. **No credit cards.**
Others may be more convivial, welcoming even, but of all the bars in this downbeat flea market square, Marcel's is the most true to life, as tatty as the traders it serves. It

stocks Cantillon Gueuze, and only seven other bars in town can boast that (*see p154* **The curse of the gueuze**). Otherwise, it's cheap beers, toasted sandwiches and heavy lunches, overseen by a statue of the Mannekin Pis decked out in local Union colours, offset by prints of the marketplace in bygone days. It's not pretty, but it's still a welcome antidote to the soullessly pretentious De Skieven Architek diagonally opposite.

La Clef d'Or

1 place du Jeu de Balle (02 511 97 62). Métro Porte de Hal/bus 20, 48. **Open** 4.30am-5pm daily. **No credit cards**.

Clock those opening hours! Yep, this is yer actual market bar, up before the larks, serving beers while traders sort out piles of toot on the square outside. Large, loud and retro, the Golden Key sports vinyl chairs and pink neon advertising signs, complemented on busy Sunday mornings by an earnest accordionist and a party atmosphere. Madame skates around in her mules and black leggings, while monsieur stands at the coffee machine barking orders to the overworked staff. He's also in charge of the *soupe du jour* pot, which means he lifts the occasional ladle. Food is otherwise of the croque monsieur and fried-egg variety.

Indigo

160 rue Blaes (02 511 38 97). Métro Porte de Hal/ bus 20, 48. **Open** hours vary. **No credit cards**.

Were it to be situated anywhere else, the Fuse would have engendered around it a whole herd of colourless pre-club designer bars from aspic to zinc. But, stuck in this grimy enclave of working-class Brussels, there is but one; not specifically pre-club, but most certainly colourful. Inside Indigo, a spangle of primary hues and glass mosaic mingles with a twinkly earring or cobalt blue designer glasses frame worn by the fashionista clientele. Locals must shield their eyes as they go past, fearing their beloved Marolles invaded by Mexican sun gods. The white furniture is pretty staid, the food solid social-worker Islington (quiche, pulses, very veggie-friendly), and big bowls of coffee are preferred over the modest choice of beers. The shape and sheen of things to come?

Recyclart

Gare de la Chapelle, 25 rue des Ursulines (02 502 57 34/café 02 289 00 59/www.recyclart.be). Métro Gare Centrale. **Open** *Café* 11am-5pm Tue-Fri, & 1hr before events. **No credit cards**.

During the day, this busy cultural centre, set amid the frescoed underpasses that divide gritty Marolles from the safety of downtown, provides sustenance for unemployed artists and single mothers. On the many events nights, the bowels of this disused railway station are transformed into a rather splendid performance and nightclub space, the daytime soup kitchen morphing into a bar buzzing with cultural types tipping ash between the neat rows of wooden tables. It's counter service only; the bar's doglegged into one corner, with a kitchen hatch at the back.

Le Renard

233 rue Haute (02 512 36 02). Bus 20, 48. **Open** 10am-9pm daily. **No credit cards**.

The Fox offers the little touches that typify Les Marolles without ever needing to stoop to the extremes of sorrow and kitsch seen in similar dives nearby (Le Petit Lion opposite, for example, specialises in framed pictures of pets long gone and frequently reminisced). Here, in a classic wood-and-mirror interior, proudly stand a Wurlitzer jukebox, a Belgian bingo machine and, occasionally, members of the local pub first XI pictured on the main wall. The room is dominated by the circular bar counter in the middle and the constant patter of neighbourhood gossip.

Walk along **rue Haute** and drop into one of the numerous Belgian beer bars. Offering no more decor than a row of wooden tables and brown walls, they give a glimpse of the real Marolles and its residents.

Beyond the Ring

Detailed in this section are the best restaurants and bars that fall outside of the central areas covered throughout the rest of this book. Some are well within the inner city, some are suburban, and others are close to the city limits; some are resolutely urban, others are countrified, taking advantage of green spaces such as the wooded parkland of the Bois de la Cambre. The Bruxellois are always willing to travel in search of rich pickings, but it's worth remembering that the city is reasonably compact and most places are reached easily by public transport or taxi.

Restaurants

Belgian & French

La Bonne Humeur

244 chaussée de Louvain, St-Josse-ten-Noode (02 230 71 69). Bus 29. **Meals served** noon-2pm, 6.30-9.30pm Mon, Thur-Sun. **Average** €€€. **Credit** MC, V.

It looks like an uninteresting proposition from the outside, just an old-style caff on one of Brussels' busiest and most unattractive roads. But this unintentionally retro resto, with its formica tables and checked floor tiles, is widely seen as purveying the best mussels and chips in Brussels ('specialité de moules' indeed). A family business for decades, it has certainly passed the test of time; folk come from far and wide to tuck into its totally unpretentious food. It's small, seating about 30, so it's wise to phone ahead, but don't be surprised if you get a friendly but firm 'complet', letting you know you've left it too late.

La Branche d'Olivier

172 rue Engeland, Uccle (02 374 47 05). Tram 55. **Meals served** noon-2.30pm, 7-11pm Mon-Thur; noon-2.30pm, 7pm-1am Fri; 7pm-1am Sat. **Average** €€€. **Credit** AmEx, DC, MC, V.

This old-style restaurant, all warm bare brick and old wooden beams, serves up a decently priced French menu. Candlelight and a rustic feel give it a warm farmhouse ambience, though the chat is loud and folk come here to kick back and relax; owner Frederick Frenays aims to make diners feel perfectly at home. It's a local crowd, by

Le Bonne Humeur. *See p146.*

and large, though folk do travel to meet up with Uccleois friends. The fine menu includes pan-fried scallops, roast rack of lamb cooked with lavender, and dorade fish in a salt crust. There is musical and/or comic entertainment at weekends and the kitchen only opens once it's finished, so phone to check times before you set out.

Les Brasseries Georges

259 avenue Winston Churchill, Uccle (02 347 21 00). Tram 23, 90. **Meals served** 11.30am-12.30am Mon-Thur, Sun; 11.30am-1am Fri, Sat. **Average** €€€€. **Credit** AmEx, DC, V.

This place has the feel of a Parisian brasserie: twisting copper and brass, vast stained windows, potted palms and statuettes of classical muses, all lurking beyond the obligatory red curtain as you walk through the doors. The kitchen specialises in crustacea: oysters, whelks, amandes and the like, brought together either as starters or a vast, dripping plateau de fruits de mer. Other dishes are more typically Belgian and French, among them andouillette, choucroute, lobster and a paving stone of steak. While Les Brasseries Georges is frequented by wealthy professionals and dignified retirees, it's generally an informal place, and folk come here not to see or be seen, but simply to eat and drink very well indeed.

Brasserie La Paix

49 rue Ropsy-Chaudron, Anderlecht (02 523 09 58).
Métro Clemenceau. **Meals served** noon-3pm Mon-Thur;
noon-3pm, 6-9pm Fri. **Average** €€. **Credit** AmEx, DC,
MC, V.

The 'Anderlecht' part of the address makes Brasserie La
Paix sound way out of town. In fact, it's only one metro
stop beyond Gare du Midi, in a multicultural microworld
vastly different to the Grand' Place area a mere ten
minutes away. Opposite the old abattoirs – now a covered
market – sits La Paix, which has been wining and dining
generations of Bruxellois since 1882. Wedding photos on
the wall bear testament to the fact that this is a friendly
place; don't be surprised if you see a waiter join a table
for a natter and a fag. The grub? Full-on Belgian, served
in an informal manner. Expect generic steaks with a
variety of sauces (the green peppercorn is wonderful),
a rib of beef for two to share, and lovely cheese croquettes.

Claude Dupont ★

46 avenue Vital Riethuisen, Ganshoren (02 426 00 00).
Métro Simonis. **Meals served** noon-2pm, 7-9.30pm
Wed-Sun. **Average** €€€€€. **Credit** AmEx, DC, MC, V.

The avuncular Claude Dupont has been the head of this
family-style restaurant for almost 30 years, during which
time he has grown to become acknowledged by locals and
Michelin (to the tune of two stars) as one of Belgium's top
chefs. The restaurant sits in a red-brick terraced
townhouse, the only clue to what lies behind the front
door a discreet white canopy bearing Dupont's name.
Inside, the family theme continues, with a living-room
feel of standard lamps, sideboards and floor-length
curtains. The kitchen prepares French-based food with
strong flavours; imaginative combinations, such as an eel
and smoked salmon mousse or beef fillet with duck foie
gras in green peppercorns, excite the palate. Three set
menus, of three, five and seven courses, cost €44-€90.

Les Deux Frères

2 avenue Vanderaey, Uccle (02 376 76 06). Bus 55.
Meals served noon-2.30pm, 7-11pm Mon-Thur;
noon-2.30pm, 7pm-midnight Fri; 7pm-midnight Sat.
Average €€€. **Credit** AmEx, DC, MC, V.

One of many upmarket, expensive restaurants in Uccle;
unsurprising, given that Uccle's an upmarket and
expensive neighbourhood. The calming, sophisticated
room is discreetly decorated with female nudes, and
discreetly served by troupes of waiters programmed to
notice a twitch of the diner's wrist towards a bottle.
Business suits and corporate entertainment clients enjoy
such deferential service, but they also like the food, drawn
from a menu big on veal, beef and fish and taking in some

If you're in
the **Woluwe
Shopping
Centre** (Métro
Rodebeek),
take the
escalator
to the lower
ground floor,
where you'll
find a food
court with
Asian noodle
bars and
small
boutiques
selling foie
gras and
fish products,
most of which
offer takeaway
food.

interesting combinations (seafood with meat) and zesty
sauces. That said, finally when your choices arrive at
your table, you may not want to attack it with the silver
cutlery, so artfully is it presented. Dress smartly.

L'Ecole

*61 rue de la Bourne, Molenbeek (02 414 21 17). Bus 63,
89.* **Meals served** noon-3pm, 6.30-10.30pm Mon-Thur;
noon-3pm, 6.30-11pm Fri; 6.30-11pm Sat. **Average** €.
Credit DC, MC, V.

School dinner, anyone? Well, kinda… Jack Jacob took
over this old school in the early 1990s, and converted it
sympathetically into a restaurant: the dining room is in
the hall, the fountain-topped terrace is where the
playground once stood, menus are on blackboards and
the tables are school-style desks. Even the old outside
loos are still in operation. Happily, the food bears little
resemblance to the soggy semolina of yore. It's chiefly
Corsican, albeit with other global influences thrown into
the mix; highlights include sardines, huge prawns, bean
stews and the ranges of imported hams and sausages that
include donkey and wild boar. A fine restaurant, though
it is located in a bit of a tatty area and probably best
reached by taxi.

Le Jardin de Nicolas

*137 avenue de Tervuren, Woluwe-St-Pierre (02 732 24
49). Métro Montgomery.* **Meals served** noon-1am daily.
Average €€. **Credit** MC, V.

The best Michelin stars

Chez Marie
Vive la France. *See p101.*

Comme Chez Soi
It's a family affair. *See p27.*

Maison du Boeuf
Michel, ma belle. *See p75.*

Au Vieux Boitsfort
Gillet: the best a man can get. *See p151.*

Restaurant Bruneau
Three-star eats. *See p150.*

La Villa Lorraine
Right said Freddy. *See p153.*

Beyond the Ring

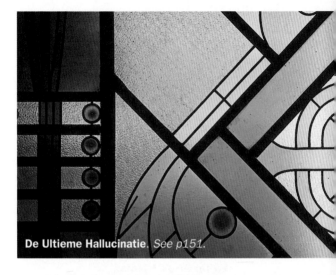

De Ultieme Hallucinatie. See p151.

Le Jardin de Nicolas is an unassuming little place frequented chiefly during the day by hungry local lunchers, including shoppers on the run from the Woluwe shopping centre, and at night by those who want a quick fix of eats before heading out for the night (or, given its late hours, for those just on their way back home with the munchies to appease). The substantial bowls of salad and pasta, plus a bargain plat du jour, serve such a clientele perfectly, as does the unpretentious atmosphere. The little garden at the front is pleasant enough, but it's also on one of Brussels' main through routes, and the ensuing noise and fumes are hardly conducive to a relaxing bite.

Restaurant Bruneau ★

75 avenue Broustin, Koekelberg (02 427 69 78). Métro Simonis. **Meals served** noon-2pm, 7-9.30pm Mon, Thur-Sun; noon-2pm Tue. **Average** €€€€€. **Credit** AmEx, DC, MC, V.

Three Michelin stars. Count 'em, then chow down on one of the finest meals you're ever likely to have. This cuisine, mustered up by innovative chef Jean-Pierre Bruneau, is seriously *haute*, and the setting in which it's served sleek, stylish and contemporary following a 1995 renovation. The menu takes in such delights as chicken stuffed with truffles, pigeon caramelised with soy, and truffled cake of brie, and the accompanying wine list is surprisingly

short but unsurprisingly well chosen. Of course, it's impossible to get a table here without booking weeks ahead, and it's also extremely pricey, but if you're going to push the boat out, you might as well do so here.

De Ultieme Hallucinatie

316 rue Royale, St-Josse-ten-Noode (02 217 06 14). Métro Botanique. **Meals served** *Restaurant* noon-2.15pm, 7-10.15pm Mon-Fri; 7-10.15pm Sat. *Café* noon-2.15pm, 6pm-midnight Mon-Fri; 6pm-midnight Sat. **Average** *Restaurant* €€€€. *Café* €. **Credit** AmEx, DC, MC, V.
Every detail in this Arts and Crafts house is in a late 19th-century style, and a visit here is a time-warp of sorts. The stylish restaurant at the front is outlandish, a dark room where rather stuffy diners take their fill of rich French-inspired food. Duck breast, côte de boeuf, stuffed Bresse chicken and slabs of turbot sum up the menu, while the chocolate desserts are thick, dark and powerful. But the prices drive some people out to the safer but blander café at the back, which serves up your more regular moules-frites-style food. Worth a visit, even if only to poke your head around the belle époque doors.

Au Vieux Boitsfort ★

9 place Bischoffsheim, Boitsfort (02 672 23 32). Tram 91. **Meals served** noon-2pm, 7-9.30pm Mon-Fri; 7-9.30pm Sat. **Average** €€€€. **Credit** AmEx, DC, MC, V.

The supermarket **Rob** (28 boulevard de la Woluwe) is the Harrods food hall of Belgium. Superb fresh and prepared food and over 1,200 wines on the racks.

A village within a city

For centuries, the *commune* of Watermael-Boitsfort to the south-east of the city centre developed as a hamlet. It's grown up considerably in relatively recent times, however, and is now a thriving suburb of Brussels. Yet the villagey feel has remained as its distinctive houses, shops and restaurants cluster around the squares of Weiner, Bischofsheim and Gilson.

The weekly highlight in Boitsfort is its Sunday market, a lively, atmospheric bustle of comings and goings that's big on flowers and food (spices, quiches, Spanish snacks, Thai goodies, farm stalls et al). Barhopping's a staple pastime here. **Au Poilu** on place Weiner is abuzz with traders such as Flemish Frank, a character who sells cooked chickens to the ready-Sunday-lunch brigade. Order a pot of Leffe from Eduardo and try his superior meat salad sandwiches. Another busy haunt is the Café du Tram, a strange place

that seems to attract the fallout from Saturday night's epic boozing.

Other establishments do decent trade the rest of the week. At the top end of the restaurant market is the Michelin-starred **Au Vieux Boitsfort** (*see p151*), while **Brasserie Antoine** (2 rue des Pêcheries), which fills to the rafters at weekends, is big on fish and seafood. Decent Italian and French brasserie food can be had at **Au Repos des Chasseurs** (11 avenue Charles Albert), though **La Dolce Vita** (13 rue Middelbourg) has a more traditionally Italian menu. And in this staunchly Belgian enclave, there's even a Tibetan restaurant in the shape of **Le Potala** (4 rue du Loutrier).

Boitsfort might be a little way out from the heart of Brussels, but it's easy to reach from the centre of town: either take the 94 tram to the end of the line or jump on a train from any of the central Brussels stations.

Beyond the Ring

In the heart of the urban village of Boitsfort sits this understated, Michelin-starred restaurant, run by chef Philippe Gillet. It's a clean, uncluttered place, a range of picture windows giving light and air to a large dining room furnished with white tables, stone-coloured armchairs and abstract art. But the food's the star. Starters include carpaccio of artichoke with shredded skate wing and preserved tomatoes, while mains such as cod with morel mushrooms and caramelised chicory, and leg of pork braised in Nice olives, offer a good impression of the modern style of French and Belgian cuisine enjoyed here. The good people of Brussels travel willingly and frequently to AVB, knowing that despite its stellar status, it's an informal and friendly restaurant.

La Villa Lorraine ★

28 chaussée de la Hulpe, Boitsfort (02 374 31 63).
Tram 94. **Meals served** noon-2pm, 7-9.30pm Mon-Sat.
Average €€€€. **Credit** AmEx, DC, MC, V.
La Villa Lorraine has been synonymous with fine dining
in Brussels for years. Its cuisine is classic French; in 1972,
the Villa became the first restaurant outside France to be
awarded three Michelin stars. It only has one now, but
don't let that stop you sampling the cooking of Freddy
Vandecasserie. Try turbot with oysters and caviar cream,
or duck liver escalopes with candied figs. Set menus make
the prices bearable, but diners here are moneyed and/or
on business (a sign genteely informs diners that 'suits are
normally worn at the Villa Lorraine'). A word, too, about
the surroundings: the Villa sits on the edge of the Bois de
la Cambre, its greenery given full range in summer.

International

Blue Elephant ★

1120 chaussée de Waterloo, Uccle (02 374 49 62).
Bus 41. **Meals served** noon-2.30pm, 7-10.30pm
Mon-Thur, Sun; noon-2.30pm, 7-11.30pm Fri; 7-11.30pm
Sat. **Average** €€€. **Credit** AmEx, DC, MC, V.

Blue Elephant

Beyond the Ring

The curse of the gueuze

The grey, sombre district of Anderlecht does not present many obvious attractions. A disgraced local football team, the house where Erasmus doodled for a while and a slaughterhouse-cum-covered market are the only draws to drag the tourist west over the Petit Ring.

But within this gloom fester genuine treasures, for the very air of Anderlecht is responsible for the most mysterious and natural of all Belgium's myriad brews. Gueuze is the world's only spontaneously fermented beer, and its most rare and sought after brand is Gueuze Cantillon, only brewed here in Anderlecht. Indeed, such is its rarity – it's the last surviving

gueuze brewery in a city where 80 once thrived – that Cantillon is ceremonially brewed for the world to witness. The brewery makes gueuze between October and May, picking a dozen days when natural fermentation will be at its most productive. The settled, gloomy climate of a sunless Anderlecht suits the process perfectly.

Attached to the Cantillon Brewery is a museum, the **Musée Bruxellois de la Gueuze** (56 rue Gheude, Anderlecht, 02 521 49 28, www.cantillon.be) unveiling the myriad mysteries of this strangest of strange brews. In a nutshell: precise amounts of wheat and barley are ground, mixed with water,

---

What started out as a small restaurant in a Brussels suburb has now become a global brand, with branches in Bangkok, Dubai, Malta and even Lyons, the heart of French gastronomy. Owned by Karl Steppe, a former antiques dealer also responsible for La Porte des Indes (*see p114*), Blue Elephant is Thai cuisine at its best. It's also Thai cuisine at its priciest, but it's worth it. The menu is big on variations of curry, with coconut milk and dollops of chilli only making an entrance when absolutely necessary. The fantastic Sunday brunch offers unlimited food for €30. It's a smart place, so dress accordingly.

Chez Julia et André

6 avenue Clemenceau, Anderlecht (02 522 73 01).
Métro Gare du Midi. **Meals served** 9am-3pm Mon-Fri.
Average €. **Credit** V.
Despite an extensive programme of renovations, the area around the Gare du Midi remains on the barren side. Yet the streets that surround it are filled with ethnic snack-bars and other small restaurants serving splendid and often keenly priced food, many of them perfect for a quick bite while waiting for a train. Chez Julia and André is one such spot. Run by a Moroccan couple, it specialises in

heated and then drained. The cooled liquid, left in barrels, reacts to microbes in the oak and in the local atmosphere, deliberately let in through vents in the roof, and ferments. The result is lambic, a flat beer served in village cafés near Brussels.

But that's not all. Two months later, the lambic begins to foam. Then – wait for it! – a couple of years later, the master brewer will, according to instinct, point his wettened finger into the open Anderlecht air. Assuming the conditions are right, lambics from a selection of barrels will be blended – in a further process too byzantine to even contemplate, let alone describe – to create the mythical gueuze. Unlike most beers, it has no sugar and no added yeast. It's a decidedly risky operation.

So what's it like? Well... anyone for tinned cider? It's an acquired taste that takes years to acquire, and one that Bruxellois have lost the habit of acquiring. In Brussels, a mere eight bars stock this authentic brew; Helsinki has 12. It doesn't help, certainly, that over-indulgence will produce the kind of hangovers that only solvent abuse can match. The curse of the gueuze, indeed. But as a few locals and more than a few Finns might testify, it's the thirst that counts.

Jewish and Middle Eastern food such as chopped liver and falafels. The menu varies daily and runs the gamut from unassuming sandwiches to steaming mains.

Passage to India

223 chaussée de Louvain, St-Josse-ten-Noode (02 735 31 47). Bus 29. **Meals served** noon-3pm, 6pm-midnight daily. **Average** €€. **Credit** AmEx, DC, MC, V.

This stretch of road, out of the centre but easy to reach, is home to a number of Indian and Pakistani restaurants, and Passage to India is one of the best. Expats come in search of British-Asian flavours – chicken madras all round – but the more traditional tandoori dishes are splendidly succulent. Kingfisher beer adds to the authenticity. It's a handsome little place, set on the ground floor of an old townhouse; choose to sit in the bustling front room, complete with bar, or in the quieter area out back. Wait staff are attentive and exceedingly polite.

Senza Nome

22 rue Royale Ste-Marie, Schaerbeek (02 223 16 17). Tram 92, 93, 94. **Meals served** noon-2pm, 7-10.30pm Mon-Fri; 7-10.30pm Sat. **Average** €€€€. **Credit** MC, V.

The name translates as 'without a name', perhaps because Senza Nome wants to escape the stereotypes usually associated with Italian restaurants. Don't come here expecting stodgy pizza or soggy lasagne: Senza specialises in earthy, flavoursome Sicilian dishes, many packing the added punch of added chilli and/or rich black olives. The branzino (a fish found mainly in Venice) comes packed with citrus flavours, the veal is powerful, and the tomatoes are almost rich enough to make a deep red meal in their own right. Do be sure to call ahead and book, especially if you're planning on coming later in the evening; once the nearby Halles de Schaerbeek empties its audience, the place fills quickly. The atmosphere can get a little smoky.

Bars

The Open

17 boulevard St-Michel, Etterbeek (02 735 49 89).
Métro Montgomery. **Meals served** 11.15am-2am daily.
Credit MC, V.
This huge brasserie/restaurant near the main roundabout of Montgomery, just east of the Parc du Cinquantenaire, attracts the bright young things of Woluwe, who flock here to pose with a cocktail or two while judging the dress sense of the latest newcomers. If this sounds like one of Dante's warmer loops of hell, so be it, but there is a strange, gilded underbelly to Brussels, and places such as this, with no paid entrance or dress code, allow open season on its observation. From time to time, someone will loosen their collar and entertain with a tune or two on the piano. The range of beers and food is in accordance with the environs.

Schievelavabo

52 rue du Collège St-Michel, Etterbeek (02 779 87 07).
Métro Montgomery. **Open** noon-3pm, 6.30pm-1am Mon-Fri. **Credit** DC, MC, V.
Capitalising on the success of the original branch, located in a traditional old house in Uccle, the Schievelavabo ('Wonky Washbasin', or – if you prefer – 'Skew-whiff Sink') brings a little bonhomie and retro conviviality to this grey residential patch stuck between the EU Quarter and Woluwe Park. Although somewhat smaller, the formula is the same: solid wooden furniture; hefty portions of classic Belgian fare; enticing options of fine local beers; dependable staff; a young, professional clientele. It would be excruciating if it were transposed to a London setting; Wimbledon, say. Here, it's a perfectly pleasant stop-off.

Take a picnic to the **Bois de la Cambre**, a countryside woodland at the bottom end of avenue Louise (tram 91, 93, 94). It's a great place for the kids to run free.

Antwerp

Eating
& drinking

in Antwerp

Eating out in Antwerp is a stylish affair for one simple reason: Antwerp itself has style. It's a city that's entirely comfortable with itself, in all its bewildering extremes: smartly turned out cultural centre on the one hand, working-class port city on the other, the space in between bridged by every manner of artistic, architectural and multicultural ideals.

In recent years, Antwerp has re-invented itself. Not since its glory days as home to Rubens and Van Dijk has it thrived so much. The city is now one of the global diamond industry's key centres, has developed into Europe's second biggest port after Rotterdam, and is having its railway station converted to accommodate the Eurostar by 2005. Antwerp is back on the map as a city where things happen.

The bar and restaurant scene here is something to text home about. From timeworn local eatery to trendy disco-dive, from traditional corner bar to Michelin-starred restaurant, it has variety to go with its quality. The locals know it and are proud of their town, believing Antwerp to be the best city in the world. That said, they aren't insular; it's in their nature to welcome outsiders. Speak French at your peril, mind: ordering in English isn't frowned on at all.

What and where

Dining and drinking in Antwerp have gone upmarket of late, and gone stylish too. To check out the new breed of local bars, head to the streets around the Royal Museum of Fine Arts (Koninklijk Museum voor Schone Kunsten) in an area commonly referred to as 't Zuid, or the South. The docks here once thrived, but for decades after, 't Zuid was badly neglected. However, when **Entrepôt du Congo** (*see p200*) opened in one of the old warehouses, other entrepreneurs followed its lead. Since the mid 1990s, 't Zuid has been transformed by new bars, a lively gay scene and some of Antwerp's more innovative restaurants, among them the late-opening **Hippodroom** (*see p184*) and **Finjan** (*see p183*).

However, the historic port hasn't broken entirely with its traditions. All over its old centre sit ancient taverns, not shy about using their history to attract tourists while providing the locals with a place to natter. The most famous is **Den Engel** (*see p199*). If you want to find out what's what in town, pull up a chair with an Antwerpenaar translator, listen and observe.

You may throw your assistant a quizzical look as you hear, loud and often, the word 'Bollocks!'. Although the perpetrators may indeed be arguing, what they're actually asking for is a glass of Antwerp's finest: De Koninck. Familiarly named 'Bolleke' after the goblet-shaped glass in which it's served, this local brew, a smooth, slightly caramelised pale ale, is ubiquitous here.

Almost equally popular is the range of grain spirits, genevers (*see p198* **High times in Flanders**). Although the Dutch disagree, Antwerp is considered to be the spiritual home of what the English adopted and adapted as gin. Certainly, as de facto capital of Flanders, Antwerp reserves a special place for its national drink.

The old town centre is home to most of Antwerp's finest restaurants, many of them in fine gabled townhouses. The design is like the cuisine: classy, stylish and modern. Sure, you'll find pizzerias and snack bars here, along with the swathe of fish restaurants for which Antwerp is rightly renowned. But, if it's serious food you're after, head to a boutique restaurant such as **Hungry Henrietta** (*see p174*).

The third area of interest to the discerning diner and barhopper in Antwerp is known as 't Eilandje, the slowly regenerating dockside area just north of the town's red light district. It's currently home to only a handful of choice establishments, but the gloomy streets around Bonaparte and William Docks will surely soon boom. If you've money to invest in hospitality, venture it here in one of the old docks buildings.

How

Attitudes in Antwerp fall into two camps. The traditional bars and older restaurants follow much the same pattern as Brussels, go-with-the-flow waiters allowing customers to casually build a tab. The upmarket restaurants have impeccable service, staff often speaking five languages. In some of the newer, trendier bars, staff tend to peer down the nose at their guests, but in general, the city is a happy-go-lucky place.

Antwerp has a compact centre, and the majority of bars and restaurants in the guide are in or within walking distance of the old town (hence, we haven't listed transport details in this chapter). Drivers should be aware that the main roads leading into the city are currently dug up and will be until around 2005, with diversions and one-way systems making driving and parking a nightmare for even the most seasoned local.

When

Restaurant hours generally follow the same pattern as Brussels. That said, eating out is a regular pastime for Antwerpenaars and we recommend that you book a table whenever possible. Most restaurants in this guide are locals' favourites, good news for you as a visitor wanting to know where the best spots are, but no fun if you can't penetrate the queues waiting to get in.

But if you're just here for the beer, you're in luck. Antwerp bars close much later than those in Brussels, and the city also has the best clubbing scene in the Benelux. Think late and you can't go wrong; especially in the summer when terrace culture kicks in and it seems the whole city is on parade.

Where to...

Restaurants

Belgian & French

Adriaan

11-13 Everdijstraat (03 231 60 35). **Meals served** noon-3pm, 6-10pm Tue-Thur; noon-11pm Fri, Sat. **Average** €€€€. **Credit** AmEx, MC, V.

Eclectic is an adjective that's wildly overused by restaurant critics. However, it's as perfect a description as you'll find for this snappily dressed eatery, housed in one of Antwerp's old gabled houses and named after Adriaan de Brouwer, a contemporary of Rubens who lived in the city. An arty theme is prominent in the layout of the numerous rooms. One is classic Burgundian, complete with grand stone fireplace and wood carvings from Mechelen; another is minimalist cream chic with black leather chairs and halogen lighting; a café space comes with a grey bar, silver candlesticks and flickable

Adriaan

For irresistible cakes and pastries, head to **Lints** (Schermerstraat 8).

Antwerp

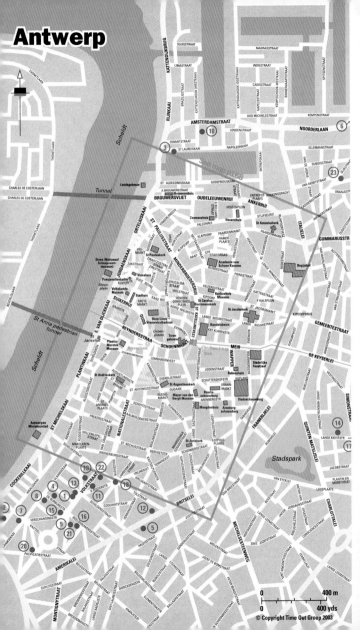

Antwerp

MAP KEY

1. The Bar Room *p194*
2. Bar Tabac *p194*
3. Cappuccino Club *p196*
4. Chilli Club *p180*
5. Ciro's *p170*
6. Dam Central *p170*
7. Entrepôt du Congo *p200*
8. Farine's Food & Future *p180*
9. Finjan *p183*
10. Fuga *p200*
11. Funky Soul Potato *p183*
12. Haddock Jazz & Food *p173*
13. Hippodroom *p184*
14. Hoffy's *p184*
15. Hopper *p201*
16. Izumi *p185*
17. Kertosono *p185*
18. Lucy Chang *p187*
19. Mogador *p204*
20. De Nieuwe Linde *p204*
21. De Scène *p207*
22. Soeki *p191*
23. De Zeste *p176*

All other Antwerp restaurants are marked on the central Antwerp map on *p168*, except Euterpia (*p172*), Minerva (*p175*), Moeskop (*p202*), P'tit Paris Services (*p179*), Het Pomphuis (*p191*), El Warda (*p193*) and Zeezicht (*p208*): all are a short distance from the centre of the city.

art books. And the menu? The 'e' word, of course, with dishes ranging from light vegetarian plates using couscous, grilled veggies and pastas through to richly classic French-inspired fish, meat and game, such as a trio of boar, hare and venison with almond croquettes.

Amadeus

20 Sint-Paulusplaats (03 232 25 87). **Meals served** 6-10.30pm Mon-Thur; 6-11.30pm Fri, Sat; 5-10.30pm Sun. **Average €. No credit cards**.

In terms of its style and atmosphere, Amadeus is a resolutely Belgian restaurant. This is deep, dark art nouveau, reclaimed from its former use as a mirror and glass factory. Long rows of wooden tables and chairs hold the secret of its success: communal eating with little regard for etiquette. A litre of house red sits plainly on the table at arrival; drink as much or as little as you like, as you're charged only for the amount you quaff. Only the food deviates from the otherwise Belgian ambience: ribs, as many as you can eat (with your fingers, naturally), served with the accompaniment of your choice (for instance, jacket spud with garlic sauce). A great buzz, and at a decent price, too.

Bernardin ★

17 Sint-Jacobstraat (03 213 07 00). **Meals served** noon-2.30pm, 6.30-10.30pm Tue-Sat. **Average €€€. Credit MC, V**.

Bernardin has made its mark as an important fine food restaurant under chef Bernard Lescrinier. The whitest and cleanest of minimal interiors, where every piece of cutlery becomes an isolated art statement, leads to an open kitchen where you can see the starched brigade preparing fine yet earthy dishes such as lamb's tongue salad, a trio of goose liver and delicately braised sweetbreads. Fish dishes are prepared with the greatest

Antwerp

Central Antwerp

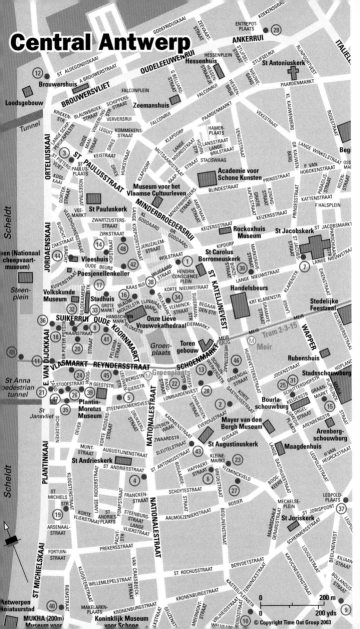

Loodsgebouw

Tunnel

Scheldt

Tunnel

Scheldt

en (Nationaal cheepvaart-museum)

Steen-plein

ANKERRUI

ENTREPOT-PLAATS

KOEKENSGRA

GODEFRIDUSKAAI

ZEEVAART STRAAT

ITALIEL

29

ST ALDEGONDISKAAI

A BROUWERSVRIET

OUDELEEUWEN RUI

Hessenhuis

HESSENPLEIN

Hessenhuis

St Antoniuskerk

12

Brouwershuis

KOENSGRACHT

BROUWERSVLIET

FALCONPLEIN

G BELLARD STRAAT

HESSEN STRAAT

HESSEN BRUG

HESSEN STRAAT

NIEUWE GANG

PAARDENMARKT

KL KAUWENBERG

PAARDENMARKT

VEKESTRAAT

RODESTRAAT

Zeemanshuis

KRIEKEN BLAUWBROEK SCHIPPERS STRAAT

ST PIETERS PAULUS PERSKAPELSTR

FALCONRUI

KLAPDOORP

HAMER-PLAATS

VENUSSTRAAT

LANGE WINKELSTRAAT

Begi

3

ST PAULUSSTRAAT

ORTELIUSKAAI

KOOL KAAI

VAN MAN WINGERD

LEGUIT

VERVERSRUI

KOMMEKENS STRAAT

KLAPDOORP

MUTSAARDSTRAAT

KLANSSTRAAT LANGE NOORDSTRAAT

HORN STRAAT

STADSWAAG

Academie voor Schone Kunsten

PRINSSTRAAT

KONING

GR OSS

P VAN HOBOKENSTRAAT

PARADIS

St Pauluskerk

VEE-MARKT

NOSESTRAAT

GOTER STRAAT

VLEESHOUWERSTRAAT

ZWARTSUSTERS STRAAT

Museum voor het Vlaamse Cultuurleven

BLINDESTRAAT

GRATIE

KAPELSTRAAT

KEIZERSTRAAT

F HALSPLEIN

Museum voor het Vlaamse Cultuurleven

JORDAENSKAAI

BURCHT

ZAKSTRAAT

MINDERBROEDERSRUI

KL GODDAARD

MINDERBROERS STR

AMBTMAN STRAAT

Rockoxhuis Museum

St Jacobskerk

LANGE NIEUWS

ST JACOBSMARKT

44

14

48

ZIRKSTRAAT

LANGE KOEPOORTSTRAAT

BR GODDAARD

KEIZERSTRAAT

MARKGRAVE

KONING

7

Vleeshuis

JERUZALEM STRAAT

St Carolus Borromeuskerk

LANGE NIEUWSTRAAT

LANGE NIEUWSTR

42

WOLSTRAAT

HENDRIK CONSCIENCE PLEIN

ST KATELIJNEVEST

Handelsbeurs

Stedelijke Feesthal

Poesjenellenkelder

17

OUDE BEURS

KAAS RUI

WIJGAARD STRAAT

1

34

KORTE NIEUWSTR

BORZE STR

LANGE NIEUWSTR

KLARENSTR

Volkskunde Museum

Stadhuis

16

GLAUW

KOEZELSTR

LIJNWAADMARKT

MEIRKANT

VLEMINCK

BEGAR DEN STR

KRT KLARENSTR

GRAMAYE STRAAT

36

32

33

GILDEKAMERS

GROTE MARKT

HANDSCHOEN MARKT

BLOMSTR

Onze Lieve Vrouwekathedraal

EIERMARKT

MEIR

MEIR

WAPPER

SUIKERRUI

8

OUDE

KOORNMARKT

Toren gebouw

MEIR BRUG

Tram 2-3-15

Meir

Rubenshuis

18

ST PIETER STRAAT

KLAARSTRAAT

41

PELGRIM STR

Groen-plaats

SCHOENMARKT

HUIDEVETTERSSTRAAT

Stadsschouwburg

49

20

VLASMARKT

E VAN DIJCKKAAI

REYNDERSSTRAAT

Groenplaats

13

GROENDAL STRAAT

Schuttershofstr

30

31

11

24

45

HOOG

LEYSSTRAAT

GR ST GEESTSTR

PAUW

GIERSTR

JOSEPH

KORTE GASTHUISSTR

Bourla-schouwburg

KELDERSTR

GRAAN MARKT

ORGEL

15

St Anna pedestrian tunnel

21

47

35

STOOFSTRAAT

39

5

STEENHOUWERSVEST

DRINK STR

LOMBARDENVEST

28

2

VLEMINCKVELD

ARENBERGSTR

Arenberg-schouwburg

Plantin-Moretus Museum

NATIONALESTRAAT

KAMMENSTRAAT

IJZEREN WAAG

ZWAARDSTR

Mayer van den Bergh Museum

Maagdenhuis

VAN ERNBO

PLANTINKAAI

MUNT STR

KORTE RIDDERS STR

AUGUSTIJNENSTRAAT

SLEUTELSTRAAT

HAPPAERT STR

KLEINE-MARKT

St Augustinuskerk

23

LANGE GASTHUISSTRAAT

LEOPOLDSTRAAT

Scheldt

St Andrieskerk

4

FRANCKEN STRAAT

STEENBURG STRAAT

ANTONIUSSTRAAT

BOGAARDE

SCHOYTESTRAAT

6

27

BREDESTRAAT

ROSIER

MECHELSE STR

KEIBERSTR

St Joriskerk

LEOPOLD PLAATS

37

ST MICHIELSKAAI

19

ST MICHIELS STR

LANGE VLIERSTRAAT

KORTE ST ANDRIES PLAATS

STEENBURG STRAAT

PACHT STR

VLIER STRAAT

NATIONALESTRAAT

AALMOEZENIERSTRAAT

BEGIJNENSTRAAT

SCHERMERSSTRAAT

ST JORISPOORT

LEOPOL

ARSENAAL STRAAT

FORTUIN STRAAT

PREKERSTRAAT

ST ROCHUSSTR

BERVOETSTRAAT

BEGIJNENVEST

KILIAAN STRAAT

BOLLANDUS

Antwerpen iniatuurstad

40

RIEMSTRAAT

MAKELAREN PLAATS

KRONENBURGSTRAAT

KASTEELPLEINSTRAAT

KAPUCINESSENSTRAAT

MUKHA (200m) Museum voor

Koninklijk Museum voor Schone

KLOOSTERSTRAAT

WILLEMLEPELSTRAAT

KRONENBURGSTRAAT

GEUZEN STR

MONTENS

VRIJHEIDSTRAAT

BOOGKEERS

9

10

© Copyright Time Out Group 2003

0 — 200 m

0 — 200 yds

care and the lightest of beurre blanc sauces; turbot is poached with a purée of blue cheese and fried spinach. It's not cheap, but a lunchtime menu makes things easier on the wallet. The restaurant is in a double house in the shadow of the St Jacob church where Rubens is buried, and a picture window looks out on to the church garden.

Brasseurs

53 Britselei (03 237 69 01). **Meals served** 9am-11.30pm Mon-Fri; 6-11.30pm Sat; 6-10.30pm Sun. **Average** €€€. **Credit** AmEx, DC, MC, V.

'Brasseurs' is French for brewers, and has proved an appropriate handle for this informal brasserie space; roll up to the round wooden tables or the long bar, where you can sit and read the papers in what amounts to a happy blend of pub and restaurant. Top of the menu are the marvellous steaks (the tournedos is the best), which come with perfect chips and a choice of sauces from béarnaise to green pepper. Also worth sampling are the bountiful salads, while the vegetarian options are usually above average. Located close to the law courts, it's frequented by legal eagles and associated professionals, plus exhausted not-guiltys desperate for a drink.

Chez Fl'Eau ★

1 Tavernierkaai (03 225 36 37). **Meals served** noon-10.30pm Mon-Thur; noon-11pm Fri; 6-11pm Sat; noon-10pm Sun. **Average** €€€. **Credit** AmEx, DC, MC, V.

Walk along the river, past or through the old storage sheds and the dock museum, and on the horizon you'll spy an old harbourmaster's house standing sternly

Antwerp

against the traffic and the big brooding sky over the River Schelde. This splendidly isolated statement was built to last, and is not about to take second place to any sissy redevelopment. Inside, the decor's loft-inspired: its rows of iron pillars wouldn't look out of place in SoHo or Wapping, though the wooden tables and yellow and blue tones are rather more conventional. The food is mostly modern takes on classic favourites, and runs to dishes such as steamed plaice with a Trappist beer sauce, onion stuffed with sweetbreads, and lamb with a cream of Noilly Prat sauce. Brilliant it is, too, with efficient service and a buzzy atmosphere only adding to the appeal. Folk clamour for a table here, so book ahead.

Ciro's

6 Amerikalei (03 238 11 47). **Meals served** 11am-11pm daily. **Average** €€. **Credit** V.

Welcome to the old school. Ciro's was decorated in 1962 and has seemingly changed little since. However, in the peculiarly circular way fashion has of repeating itself, its 40-year-old fixtures and fittings are stylish once again, their authenticity further furnishing their credibility. The clientele, many of them also decorated à la 1962, come to Ciro's chiefly for the steaks, widely regarded as the best in Antwerp. That said, the home-made croquettes stuffed with melted cheese or tiny shrimps are a real highlight. Waitresses schlep around the place without ceremony, and the diners take a similarly no-nonsense approach to eating. However, while this is something of a local institution, don't feel that as a visitor you'll be out of place; everyone gets a warm welcome, and hapless foreigners will also get treated to a well-meaning tour of the menu.

Dam Central

27 Damplein (03 226 33 13). **Meals served** noon-2pm, 6-10pm Mon-Fri; 6-10pm Sat. **Average** €€€. **Credit** AmEx, MC, V.

On arrival, it looks a little run down and lonely, an old station booking hall with a railway embankment behind it and old newspapers blowing across the windy square at the front. But Dam Central has a light and modern feel inside, all the better to suit its all-things-to-all-people usage as café, bar, restaurant and even gallery. However, it's the restaurant part of the operation that dominates, with its exciting French-inspired menu designed to titillate the younger tastebud. Example dishes? Fried scallops and black pasta with beurre blanc; tournedos of salmon with broccoli and carrot mousse and a soft mustard sauce. Chunky chips de la casa make a perfect accompaniment to the slabs of Argentinean beef. Music moves from lounge to Latin to soft house.

For a drink or meal with an uninterrupted view across the river of the Antwerp skyline, head through the foot tunnel to the **Royal Yacht Club** (Thonetlaan 133, 03 219 27 84).

Amadeus. *See p167*.

Désiré de Lille

14-18 Schrijnwerkerstraat (03 232 62 26). **Meals served** *May-Sept* 9am-10pm daily. *Oct-Apr* 9am-8pm daily. **Average €. No credit cards**.

This grande dame has a genteel 1930s look about it, its big windows opening up to the street and its interior filled with banquettes and first-class railway carriage lights. Here, ladies slip off their coats but leave on their hats and scarves as they tuck in to Belgian waffles, fruit-filled beignets (similar to doughnuts) and laquements (a thin waffle with syrup); another speciality is the smoutebollen, a beignet without fruit. The kitchen is open to both restaurant and street – this place has nothing to hide – while a vast glass pergola at the back leads into a rather magnificent garden. That Désiré is a great blend of the old style and the new wave is perfectly illustrated by the broad mix of people who come here.

Euterpia

De 3 Fluwelen
24 Hofstraat (03 234 05 27). **Meals served** noon-2pm,
6-10pm Tue-Fri; 7-10pm Sat. **Average** €€€€.
Credit AmEx, MC, V.
Quiet, classy and sophisticated, this old house bang in
the centre of town is the place to go for an old-fashioned
romantic dinner. The contrast between the great wooden
door and the clean interior works as decent foreplay for
what is to come; choose from the white library or the
orangery, then be seated on deeply padded chairs with
white tie-backs. The service is discreet and gentle, and
the food fine enough to melt the most stubborn of
potential *amours*: pink lamb in red reductions, softly
steamed fish in lemons and creams and the like. By the
way, 'fluwelen' means velvet. Go figure.

Euterpia ★
2 General Capiaumontstraat, Berchem (03 236 83 56).
Meals served 7-11pm Wed-Sat; 6.30-10pm Sun.
Average €€€€. **Credit** AmEx, MC, V.

For a quick
Thai bite, try
snack-resto
Khun Lung
(Vlasmarkt
7, 03 225
16 87).

Antwerp

The area known as Cogels Osylei is perhaps the most perfect area in which to experience archetypically Belgian art nouveau and neoclassical architecture. Great 19th-century houses line many of the streets, and four such properties sit on the area's central roundabout, known for this reason as the Four Seasons. It is among this splendid setting that you will find the imposing Euterpia, a fine restaurant that appeals to the well-heeled, thick-walleted set. Outside stands a statue of its namesake, a Roman muse to music, as wrought-iron gates lead to a classical garden. The food has a lightness about it, and sings with freshness and balance: a vol-au-vent filled with Mechelse koekoek (a free range bird) is not smothered in a thick sauce, but married with tender sweetbreads and truffle juice, while grilled lobster arrives with fresh pasta glistening with basil oil.

't Fornuis ★

9 Haarstraat (03 231 32 07). **Meals served** noon-2pm, 7-10pm Tue-Fri; 7-10pm Sat. **Average** €€€€. **Credit** AmEx, DC, MC, V.

Chef-owner Johan Segers has won a Michelin star for this small two-storey operation, located in a listed corner building near the docks and widely regarded as one of Antwerp's finest (and most expensive) restaurants. It's an elegant and formal place, decorated with a mix of antiquey fixtures and modern art, but without a menu in sight. Instead, Segers and his staff will take you patiently through the day's offerings, which could include truffles, foie gras, turbot or game. It veers towards the formal end of the market – head here to impress or to be impressed – and is frequented by a great many business types on expense accounts. But if you're planning a gastronomic tour of Antwerp, 't Fornuis should be on it.

Haddock Jazz & Food

8 Amerikalei (03 237 78 01). **Meals served** noon-2.30pm, 6-10pm Mon, Wed-Fri; 6-10pm Sat, Sun. **Average** €€€. **Credit** V.

Occupying a belle époque corner house, this strangely named restaurant is a classy, Frenchy mix of brasserie and jazz bar. The bar dominates, filled as it is with glasses and bottles of every drink known to man and posters advertising varieties of French booze. A layer of loucheness is created by the purple tablecloths and leopardskin lampshades, which combine to give it an art deco cruise liner feel, and the pianist who tinkles on Mondays and Thursdays. The menu is not especially startling – roast cod, wild duck, saddle of hare, all dressed in various sauces – but it is well executed by chef Demsey Bossuyt in a typically Belgian way. The presence of a cigar bar makes it a smoking zone, but without the fug it wouldn't really be jazz.

Antwerp

Hungry Henrietta

19 Lombardenvest (03 232 29 28). **Meals served** noon-2pm, 6-9pm Tue-Fri; 6-9pm Sat. **Average** €€€. **Credit** AmEx, DC, MC, V.

Don't wear that trendy little black frock or your black Paul Smith suit when you dine here. You might well disappear into the background. Everything in this daring space – walls, tables, chairs – is black, including the clothes of the refined Antwerpenaars who dine here. Oliver Cielen has been preparing modern Belgian food in the same way as his parents might have done three decades ago: perfectly balanced skate wing with black butter, salmon fillet with endive, quail nestling on a bed of herby salad, melting roasted leg of lamb with rosemary and classic desserts of the choccy mousse variety. It's good value and, given the decor, surprisingly friendly and informal.

De Kleine Zavel. *See p175.*

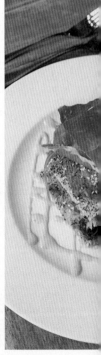

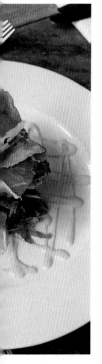

De Kleine Zavel ★

2 Stoofstraat (03 226 21 90). **Meals served** noon-2pm, 6-10.30pm Mon-Thur; noon-2pm, 6.30-11pm Fri; 6.30-11pm Sat; noon-2pm, 6-10.30pm Sun. **Average** €€€. **Credit** MC, V.

The restaurant of the moment: a blend of outstanding food, impeccable service and a deliciously informal atmosphere. The latter is built on the bistro-style decor; you'll be seated in a long, distressed room among old beer and wine crates, eating from unclothed tables. But the former comes from a menu, created by young chef and owner Carlo Didden, that knocks such an unassuming image on its arse: treat yourself to three scallops prepared in independent styles, or to a rare fillet of hare with wild mushroom ravioli and a teacup of truffle broth, with a slice of foie gras on the side. This only leaves the service, which comes courtesy of waiters able to describe the day's specials in Dutch, English, French and German with a confident flair. Inventive, up-to-the-minute and totally without pretension: don't miss it.

Mares

2 Kelderstraat (03 226 30 33). **Meals served** 11.30am-11pm Mon-Thur; 11.30am-midnight Fri, Sat. **Average** €€. **Credit** AmEx, DC, MC, V.

Located opposite the Bourla theatre, Mares serves up a sexy menu to a young crowd and A-list gays. With its black leather seats and chandeliers big enough to swing from, it's camp, perhaps even over-the-top, but the food is great and priced very reasonably. To start, try spicy goat cheese croquettes or spring roll filled with chicken, honey, leek and dates; to follow, orange-marinated pork fillet with red cabbage and figs or stir-fried scampi with noodles. Mares' menu unashamedly borrows from all over the world and the insatiable crowd just can't get enough of it; unless you book you could be fighting for a seat. It's related to the more informal Kleine Bourla (*see p202*) next door, even sharing the same kitchen.

Minerva

36 Karel Oomsstraat (03 216 00 55). **Meals served** noon-2pm, 6.30-9.30pm Tue-Sat. **Average** €€€€. **Credit** AmEx, DC, MC, V.

In the early 20th century, Minerva was a famous and rather glitzy Belgian automotive marque, known as 'the car of kings and queens'. This restaurant occupies an old Minerva garage as part of a luxurious art deco hotel, though that's where the connection ends. The room has been stripped to its bare bricks and done out in a Habitat style, the glass-covered mechanic pits being the only real clue to its previous life. The cooking can best be described as modern Belgian, and takes in such heartily tempting dishes as mussels cooked in a mustard cream. It's a popular place, though its hotel location means it's mainly used by out-of-towners.

Sir Anthony Van Dyck

16 Oude Koornmarkt (on Vlaaikensgang) (03 231 61 70). **Meals** *Sittings* noon-1.30pm, 6.30-7pm & 9-9.30pm Mon-Sat. **Average** €€€. **Credit** AmEx, DC, MC, V.
You'll need to really search for this place, tucked away at the end of a narrow blind alley. If you stick with it, you'll eventually reach a building that resembles a 16th-century dolls' house, tiny, inviting and impeccably decorated with antiques and tasteful soft furnishings. The food's not bad, either: seafood, fish and finely cooked fillets of veal will arrive in true Belgian-sized portions. Note the opening times: food is served at three sittings only, though you are welcome to spend as much time you like in the bar. If you're lucky, you'll hear the carillon ringing out from the cathedral, just as Van Dyck himself would have over 350 years ago.

De Zeste ★

36 Lange Dijkstraat (03 233 45 49). **Meals served** noon-2pm, 7-9pm Mon, Tue, Thur-Sat; noon-2pm Wed. **Average** €€€€€. **Credit** AmEx, DC, MC, V.
The setting may be a little suburban-looking, but make no mistake about it: Marc Clement has created a real haven of gastronomy in the centre of Antwerp. The food here is modern, innovative and pleasingly fuss-free: truffles dot a pigeon breast in a cream of Anjou sauce; exquisitely simple lobster bisque comes with five subtle levels of flavour. There is no menu; instead, Clement will arrive at your table and describe what he found at the market that morning and what he intends to do with it. The approach allows for a large measure of surprise and even shock, though it's worth bearing in mind that the bill may be larger than you expected.

Le Zoute Zoen

17 Zirkstraat (03 226 92 20). **Meals served** noon-2.30pm, 6-10pm Tue-Thur, Sun; noon-2.30pm, 6-11pm Fri; 6-11pm Sat. **Average** €€€. **Credit** AmEx, MC, V.
The 'salty kiss' is considerably more romantic than its name suggests. Deep red and bare brick walls allow candlelight to play loving tricks in the warm and luscious interior, as bunches of dried flowers give a rustic charm. Chef Viviane Verheyen serves up a mainly fishy blend of Franco-Belge food, with the occasional Italian twist. Mussels are cooked in tomato and shallots and grilled with garlic butter, in a modern take on classic escargots; red mullet comes with ratatouille. Meat-eaters will be delighted with the baked veal sweetbreads with bacon and sweet pear dressing, while vegetarians usually enjoy

Fill a wooden crate with Belgian and imported cheese at **Vervloet** (Wiegstraat 28).

a mighty bruschetta smothered in wild mushrooms. On Saturday evenings, there are two sittings, ending or beginning at 9pm.

Fish & seafood

Maritime

4 Suikerrui (03 233 07 58). **Meals served** *Jan-June* noon-2pm, 6-10pm Mon, Tue, Fri; noon-10pm Sat, Sun. *July-Dec* 6-10pm Mon, Thur; noon-2pm, 6-10pm Tue, Fri; noon-10pm Sat, Sun. **Average** €€€€. **Credit** AmEx, MC, V.

Just beyond the Grote Markt and just before the river, you'll find a welter of seafood restaurants that cater to the tourist trade. Locals will advise you to steer clear of them (as, for what it's worth, does this guide). However, tucked in among the dross is one eatery worthy of a visit, a true petunia in an onion patch. Maritime is so deeply Belgian in its look – wooden beams, candle lightbulbs, red tablecloths – it could almost be a film set. The food is just as classic, with a menu that leans heavily towards eels (not just in green sauce, but also in cream or fried in butter à la meunière, as if they were Dover sole) and mussels. The fresh croquettes stuffed with prawns are fantastic.

De Matelote ★

9 Haarstraat (03 231 32 07). **Meals served** noon-2pm, 7-10pm Tue-Fri; 7-10pm Sat. **Average** €€€€. **Credit** AmEx, DC, MC, V.

The best   Minimalist decor

Absoluut Zweeds
Home Swede home. *See p179.*

Adriaan
Eclectic dreams. *See p165.*

Fuga
Docks away. *See p200.*

Hippodroom
Woodn't it be good. *See p184.*

Soeki
Wash and go. *See p191.*

Wok a Way
Asia minor. *See p193.*

Antwerp

P'tit Paris Services.
See p179.

The Sailor is no Jack Tar of a restaurant: this very able seaman wears epaulettes, and has gold braid all around his toque. Chef Didier Garnich takes his shopping trolley to market each morning to pick the shiniest fish and vegetables, and then sets to preparing his menu for the day; expect to find such enticing combinations as baked sole with pistou and pine nuts. Despite the sky-high prices, the place is always packed – well, it does only have a dozen tables – and the locals refer to it in hushed tones as the best fish and seafood restaurant in the city. Foreigners find it frequently via its one-starred mention in the Michelin guide.

Het Nieuwe Palinghaus

14 Sint-Jansvliet (03 231 74 45). **Meals served**
noon-2.30pm, 6-10pm Wed-Sun. **Average** €€€.
Credit AmEx, DC, MC, V.

The tables at Het Nieuwe Palinghaus are separated by a
steering wheel taken from a boat, which rather gives the
game away about what to expect from this fine restaurant;
assuming, that is, that the sepia prints of 19th-century
Antwerpenaars fishing their cotton smocks off haven't
already done so. Eels in green sauce are a Flemish
favourite, and are one of the specialities of the house;
another is the restaurant's own take on the classic
bouillabaisse, using seasonal fish from either cold or warm
waters. When you bear in mind that fish is generally an
expensive option in Antwerp these days, the food at the
New Eel House is very good value; unsurprising, then, that
it should be packed more or less constantly.

P'tit Paris Services ★

41-45 Lange Lobroekstraat (03 272 52 72). **Meals
served** noon-3pm, 6-10pm Mon, Tue, Thur, Fri; noon-3pm
Wed; 6-10pm Sat. **Average** €€€. **Credit** MC, V.

P'tit Paris Services is located in a former animal
slaughterhouse, and – from the hose-down white-tiled
walls to the overhead tracks from which hang carcass
hooks – the owners don't let you forget it. It's a dead
trendy place and you'll need to book, but it'll more than
likely be worth it. The blackboard menus – hung, in a
brilliant touch, from the carcass hooks, and whizzed
around on the tracks to each individual table – will detail
dishes taking in the likes of swordfish, whole lobster,
oysters, crab, eels and soups served by the litre. The
peculiar name comes from the fact that P'tit Paris
Services is also a supplier to other restaurants and runs
a catering service from the premises.

International

Absoluut Zweeds

12 Wijngaardstraat (03 237 28 43). **Meals served**
noon-2pm, 6-10pm daily. **Average** €€€. **Credit** MC, V.

It may have only recently moved from a location in
which it had been based for four years, but Absoluut
Zweeds, aka Absolutely Swedish, has remained
absolutely stylish in the upheaval, all Arne Jacobsen
chairs and sleek bleached woods. The descriptions of the
dishes reflect the crystalline clarity of the design; try
Black and White, tuna and sole with a black and white
sauce made from winter truffles and a cappuccino of
forest mushrooms with garlic froth. *Varsågod*! If it all
makes you snowblind, let the menus do the work: the
teaming of dishes on them is impeccable.

There's a
wild range of
chocolates at
Burie (Korte
Gasthuisstraat
3): a train
complete
with steam,
a Swiss watch
with dolls that
pop out on
the hour…

Broers van Julienne ★

45-47 Kasteelpleinstraat (03 232 02 03). **Meals
served** noon-10pm Mon-Sat; 6-10pm Sun. **Average** €€.
Credit MC, V.

A truly classy place, this vegetarian restaurant has a
timeless, reading-room atmosphere and – in summer –
a becalmed garden that's a genuine oasis amid the hubbub
of Antwerp city life. All the food is prepared using natural
and biologically-sane ingredients. Middle Eastern
influences creep in with Moroccan salads and a tagine
with dorade. The fact that fish edges onto the menu, for
those who need the protein, illustrates that Broers van
Julienne has recognised that many people now eschew
red meats but don't necessarily fancy a life of legumes
and pulses. The attached shop sells deli-quality foods and
wine, while the takeaway-only bakery department merits
special mention: we can heartily recommend the
sublimely squidgy chocolate, cream and cherry cake. The
perfect place if you're in mixed carnivorous and
vegetarian company.

Chilli Club

43 de Burburestraat (03 248 90 90). **Meals served**
noon-2.30pm, 5-10.30pm Mon-Fri; 5-11pm Sat; noon-10pm
Sun. **Average** €€. **Credit** MC, V.

The two-metre-tall red chilli outside the sidestreet
entrance of this cantina – a modern place that describes
itself as an Asian brasserie – acts as a visual beacon for
lovers of hot stuff. This is a serious place, too: each dish
is given a figure on the Scoville scale, Wilbur Scoville
being the American chemist who devised a grading
system for chilli strength in 1912. The small menu
includes some exciting concepts, among them Asian
tapas, little sushi rolls and wun tuns, a fiercely hot Thai
red beef salad (at 1,000 on the Scoville scale, it's not for
the faint-hearted), and an assortment of stir-fries, noodle
dishes and CC specials involving rice, tempura,
vegetables and tofu. But running through it all is the
small red demon ready to blow both mind and mouth.

Farine's Food & Future

40 Vlaamsekaai (03 238 37 76). **Meals served** 7-10pm
Mon, Wed-Sun. **Average** €. **No credit cards**.

A long scrubbed pine table with room to seat around 20
is the centrepiece of this small and slightly bizarre
cantina. At one end is what appears to be a grandmother's
kitchen, and the homely theme continues with great
yellow jugs of milk and sugar bowls left along the length
of the table. It's doubtful, of course, that you'll find many
such cosy residential houses with a psychedelic mural on
the wall, but the decor doesn't detract too much from the
small international menu, which offers such dishes as red

For the best
cheesecake
in the world
(probably),
head to the
Jewish bakery
Kleinblatt
(Provincie-
straat 206),
there since
1903.

Farine's Food & Future.
See p180.

curried scampi, nasi goreng and tabouleh, the latter one of a decent selection of veggie meals. It also makes ace doorstep sandwiches, and serves a fry-up breakfast all day to customers who sit and philosophise as funky music thumps quietly in the background. From 5pm on Mondays, staff 'empty the fridge': all dishes go for €7.

Fez

52 Kloosterstraat (03 288 63 18). **Meals served** 6-11pm daily. **Average** €€. **Credit** AmEx, MC, V.
The first thing you'll notice on entering Fez is the vast clay pot, big enough to hold not just Ali Baba but all 40 of the thieves. Indeed, there's something of *The 1,001 Nights* about this theatrical place, all twinkling lights and Middle Eastern lanterns. Fez buzzes all the time, packed out with party people telling their own stories in loud voices. The food – vast plates of Moroccan meze, traditional tagines packed with chicken, honey and baked

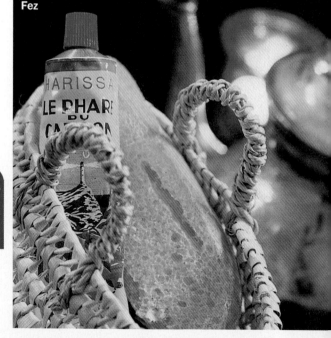

Fez

vegetables – is predictable, but it's also honest, and you won't leave feeling dissatisfied. Come here to start an evening and it'll set you up for the night; come here for the night and it'll set you up for the morning. Irrepressible, loud and fun, but even a genie can't help you get a table if you don't book.

Finjan

1 Graaf van Hoornestraat (03 248 77 14). **Meals served** 11am-4am Mon-Thur, Sun; 11am-5am Fri, Sat. **Average €. No credit cards.**

Located right next door to the Royal Museum of Fine Arts, this Middle Eastern eathouse offers a predictable but undeniably tasty selection of shoarmas, falafels, couscous, rich Mediterranean stews and Israeli specials (the chicken soup is a treat). During the day, Finjan pulses with local workers and folk needing to rest their feet after a long cultural trawl, but at night, students and multi-cultural locals show up, and the place rocks with loud conversation. In summer, the corner plot outside is packed with tables, which are then packed with diners. Put your feet up and tuck in: everyone else does.

Funky Soul Potato

76 Volkstraat (03 257 07 44). **Meals served** noon-10.30pm Tue-Sun. **Average €. No credit cards.**

This tidy, tiny corner caff certainly lives up to the first part of its name: its interior is dominated by purple and lime green, with diners left to sit on plastic chairs from the 1950s. It fills the brief of the last word, too: the menu is dominated by spuds, especially the jacket potatoes that are served with a raft of imaginative fillings. Not much sour cream here, thankfully; instead, tuck into spuds filled with chilli beef, char-grilled vegetables or creamy chicken. The names are a hoot: Free Willy (fish, not whale), Funkadelic and Ooh Poo Pah Doo. Wash everything down with a house cocktail or a reasonably priced glass of beer or wine. Staff, atmosphere and music are all pretty laid back, which is just how the local young, arty and somewhat studenty clientele like it.

Gringo's Cantina

24 Ernest van Dijckkaai (03 232 63 84). **Meals served** 6-11.30pm Wed-Sun. **Average €. No credit cards.**

At 5.50pm, go and join the orderly queue waiting for Gringo's to open. This tiny cantina doesn't take reservations, but has proved very popular with locals in search of cheap, cheerful and strawberry Margaritas. Because of its size, it restricts groups to six people, so don't expect to get in if you're with a tourist bus-load. There won't be a table free when you arrive, but sit at the bar and wait: the turnaround is fast. The menu is made up of perfectly decent Mexican staples: enchiladas,

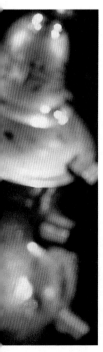

tortillas, quesadillas and hearty salads, with dessert choices running from chocolate mousse to… actually, just chocolate mousse. Combine a meal here with a beer along the road at Café Beveren (*see p195*) and you'll have seen Antwerp in a light both weird and wonderful.

Hippodroom ★

10 Leopold de Waelplaats (03 248 52 52). **Meals served** noon-2.30pm, 6.30-11pm Mon-Fri; 6.30-11pm Sat, Sun. **Average** €€€. **Credit** AmEx, MC, V.

Hippodroom's long, slender dining room contrasts perfectly with its turn-of-the-century exterior, a 1904 house immediately opposite the Royal Museum of Fine Arts. Massive works of art and photographs, mounted on coolly coloured walls, look over a slim line of minimally set tables perched on wooden floors. It's a chic place, albeit in a retro-'60s-Scandinavian way, and its confident aesthetic style extends to the international menu: Iranian caviar, sushi, French-inspired nibbles such as fillet of lamb with truffle risotto, and vegetarian options including aubergine lasagne. The garden gives an alluring glow to the overall sensual ambience in the summer. It's not cheap, but what price love?

Hoffy's

52 Lange Kievitstraat (03 234 35 35). **Meals served** 11am-10pm Mon-Thur, Sun; 11am-3pm Fri. **Average** €€. **Credit** AmEx, DC, MC, V.

In the heart of Antwerp's Jewish Quarter sits Hoffy's, a classic kosher restaurant that dishes up fine versions of all the usual staples: latkes and cholent, matzo ball soup and chopped liver. However, Hoffy's catering and import-export business has helped it gain a reputation with indigenous Antwerpenaars who've taken a shine to the Ashkenazi cuisine (big in central Europe). Kreplach are similar in appearance to ravioli, but are actually noodle dumplings stuffed with chopped meat or cheese, simmered in broth and used as an accompaniment for soup. A tzimmes, meanwhile, is a slow-cook casserole, traditionally served at Rosh Hashanah using salt beef, vegetables and sweeteners of fruit or honey plus a touch of cinnamon. Hoffy's also does takeaway.

Izumi ★

14 Beeldhouwersstraat (03 216 13 79). **Meals served** noon-2pm, 6.30-10.30pm Tue-Sat. **Average** €€€€.
Credit AmEx, DC, MC, V.
Izumi has been nestling in its old Antwerp townhouse since 1978, and over the last quarter-century has developed an unassailable reputation as the best Japanese restaurant in the city. Dutch chef-owner Ed Balke spent four years mastering the art of Japanese food preparation, and in 1999 teamed up with Takeati Kato, a sushi chef from Hiroshima. The result is pure Japanese culinary art, prepared in the time-honoured fashion and heavy on the fish and seafood: belly of tuna, fried eel with cucumber, squid, octopus and urchin, marinated seaweed, full spreads of sushi, sashimi and teriyaki. If you find it difficult to choose from the carte, the range of set menus (€36-€52) ought to make life easier.

Karper

14 Vlasmarkt (03 770 85 86). **Meals served** 6-10pm Mon, Thur-Sun. **Average** €€€. **Credit** AmEx, DC, MC, V.
When Jeroen Ensing opened Karper, he brought a fresh feel to a traditional area. That said, the design is surprisingly sober for a new-breed restaurant. The Mediterranean-influenced menu changes according to season, and goes into great detail about each dish. Just as well, too: the intriguing combinations test even the most seasoned foodie. Sashimi can come up à la provençale; pheasant, baked with chicory, is teamed with a foie gras sauce; fish in the shape of young turbot is served with a tomato risotto; and eels are done in the Japanese style, caramelised with sweet and sour cucumber. Matching wines to this lot could be a little tricky, but Ensing's list of mostly New World wines has been chosen with aplomb.

Kertosono ★

118 Provinciestraat (03 225 02 14). **Meals served** 6-10pm Wed-Sun. **Average** €€. **No credit cards**.
This shoebox Indonesian restaurant, whose interior is filled with heavy parasols and tiny twinkling lights and whose garden is done out in Balinese fashion, is a little

Dokter Marcus
(Nationalestraat 99) sells game, poultry and rabbit, just right for stewing in Belgian beer.

joy. The speciality of the house is, of course, the rice table
(€30), a large spread of freshly cooked dishes designed
for sharing and taking in the ubiquitous nasi goreng,
made with prawns and egg. Belgian owner Dirk dresses
in traditional Indonesian outfits at the weekend, a

Kertosono. *See p185*.

reminder of his love for the country and his chef Gigi, who does a good job of the cooking. Kertosono is permanently popular, so do book, especially if you want a garden table during the summer months.

Lombardia

78 Lombardenvest (03 233 68 19). **Meals served** 7.30am-6pm Mon-Sat. **Average €. No credit cards**.
This little canteen sits in the middle of a busy pedestrianised shopping area, a spark of eccentricity that brings a little light and colour to an otherwise drearily typical high-street scene. Tiny, with close-packed tables cluttering up the shop space, this organic café offers an impressive array of warm and cold sandwiches, salads, organic cakes and bread to either eat in, take away or, during the milder months, eat out on the terrace. The whole operation, fun and funky in feel, represents a nice break from normality, not least because kids are made to feel more than welcome. Who said health food has to be boring?

Lucy Chang

17 Marnixplaats (03 248 95 60). **Meals served** noon-midnight daily. **Average €€. No credit cards**.
The first thing you'll see upon entering Lucy Chang is an oriental market-stall, to the right of which is sited a long, low bar. The kitchen at the back is partly visible, but the curtain that screens it helps give this Thai and Malaysian restaurant an eastern feel. The tables are set simply, with paper napkins and chopsticks, but this is no oriental theme-park; rather, it's a slick and modern operation, albeit one with just the right amount of tradition attached. The menu mixes fierce Thai curries, made with seafood, fish and chicken, with the milder nut-based stir-fries and satays of Malaysia. The approach is no-nonsense and street food-market, and if you let your imagination loose, you could forget you're in Antwerp.

Las Mañas

36 Ankerrui (03 231 72 20). **Meals served** noon-3pm, 6.30-10.30pm Mon-Sat. **Average €€€. Credit** MC, V.
The entry in the Antwerp *Yellow Pages* for this Spanish restaurant declares: 'No Publicity Necessary!' An Antwerp institution since its beginnings in 1972 and run by the family Espantoso, Las Mañas attracts not only the Spanish community, but Antwerpenaars seeking some sunshine and sangria. The menu is serious: giant gambas cooked in sherry or with a garlic cream sauce, squid, sardines, paella, zarzuela, swordfish, this, that and the other served a la plancha. Saturday is family day: crowds turn out in their best gear and sing as the paella is brought to the table, overflowing with chicken, rabbit and

seafood. You wouldn't think that you could find such a *playa* feeling in the middle of Antwerp, but it really is the best thing this side of the Pyrenees.

Mangia e Bevi ★

25 Lange Nieuwstraat (03 213 26 13). **Meals served** 6.30-10pm Mon-Sat. **Average** €€€€. **Credit** MC, V.

This is no ordinary Italian dive. Mangia e Bevi is one of Antwerp's most endearing and enduring restaurants, classy and stylish with regional menus that knock spots off your average trattoria. Dario, the main man, had the great idea to open a restaurant that served up food based on his mother's fantastic home cooking. But where to find a chef to recreate such quality? 'Ah, I know!' said Dario… and flew in his mamma, Maria. Her exquisite and robust dishes originate mainly from the Italian south, but each month, a special three-course menu (€30) offers up a series of specialities from a different part of the country. Dario himself shoots off to Italy on a regular basis to buy the first-class ingredients: meat, sausages, cold cuts and cheeses, with a 400km detour for the gorgonzola alone. As the saying goes, book ahead to avoid disappointment.

The best Conversions

Amadeus
Formerly a glass factory. *See p167.*

Chez Fl'Eau
A longtime dock house. *See p169.*

Dam Central
Once a railway booking hall. *See p170.*

De Kleine Zavel
Used to be a hotel breakfast room. *See p175.*

Minerva
Housed in an ex-garage. *See p175.*

Het Pomphuis
In a dry dock pump house. *See p191.*

P'tit Paris Services
Previously a slaughterhouse. *See p179.*

Soeki
Located in a launderette. *See p191.*

Antwerp

La Piada

77 Hoogstraat (03 288 63 72). **Meals served** 11am-8pm Wed-Sun. **Average** €. **No credit cards**.

Located opposite the entrance to the foot tunnel under the river, this little Italian place is a welcoming stop for those piling through, its tiny, rough-Artexed room inviting and informal, the blackboard plastered into the wall making no fuss of the day's specials. Piada and piadina are Italian peasant breads, a kind of cross between pitta bread and pizza dough baked on a device called a testo. The testo here is what filling to choose: all the breads here are served piping hot and crammed with cheese, ham, sausage, tomato and other pizza-esque toppings. One classic is the piadana Romagnola, which comes with wafer-thin Parma ham, but whichever one you pick, it'll be perfect for lunch or an early evening bite. You shouldn't miss the coffee or the tiramisu, either: the former rich, the latter gluggy, soft and sensuous. All told, this is an Italian restaurant with a difference; if it's spagbol you're after, head elsewhere.

La Piada

Het Pomphuis.
See p191.

Antwerp

Foodmakers
(Meir 10, 03 226 60 69) is a sandwich bar in the same vein as Pret A Manger. Head here for triangular home-made English sandwiches.

Het Pomphuis ★

Droogdok, 7 Siberiastraat (03 770 86 25). **Meals served** 11am-2.30pm, 6-11pm Mon-Fri; 11am-11pm Sat, Sun. **Average €€€. Credit** AmEx, DC, MC, V.

The renovation of the docks area moves on apace. This magnificent old building was once the pump-house for the dry dock, but was converted in early 2003 into an equally magnificent restaurant. The massive arched windows and lofty ceilings whisper of a time when these places were built as cathedrals to the industrial age. Now, crisply laid tables sit as icons of the new age, Parisian globes and industrial lamps throwing light on the ironwork and stone stairs. The menu is unusual for Antwerp: Pacific Rim with Asian influences. A goat's cheese salad comes with dates, apple and beetroot syrup and a Thai thyme vinaigrette, or Chinese barbecued pork with noodles, ketchup and coriander. For those who prefer to remain closer to home, try cod with chicory purée, a poached egg and sauce mousseline. If this place is anything to go by, Antwerp's docklands have a future.

Sjalot en Schanul

12 Oude Beurs (03 233 88 75). **Meals served** 9am-8pm Mon, Tue, Thur-Sun. **Average €. No credit cards**.

One of those hidden places that only locals seem to know about. An initial glimpse tells the eye it's looking into a greengrocer's; however, look a little closer and you'll see a small glass counter at the back, and some simple tables set for lunch. Sit down among the racks of vegetables and try one of the thick hearty soups on offer, such as farmhouse veg with chunks of organic bread. If you're a fish-eater, take a hulking great salad with avocado and smoked salmon. Sandwiches, toasts and pasta dishes are also on offer, the many vegetarian options made using the same vegetables that are on sale. It can be a bit disconcerting when someone comes in to shop, but you'll soon get used to it.

Soeki

21 Volkstraat (03 238 75 05). **Meals served** 6-11pm Tue-Thur; 6pm-midnight Fri-Sun. **Average €. No credit cards**.

Soeki is the name of an old launderette chain in Belgium, but it's become common usage for a wash-house in much the same way that ridding your house of dust with a vacuum cleaner is commonly called Hoovering. This restaurant is located in an old Soeki, though the machines and dryers have been replaced by a washed-up retro look all its own (low-slung tables, arty installations). The food takes in tapas, sushi, Moroccan and Middle Eastern meze, Indonesian rices and more, all in snack-and-share portions. The buzz comes from its informality, and its

Antwerp

Spuds-u-like

Sure, it's slap bang in the centre of town, right next to the Grote Markt. However, the real reason **Frituur Number One** (Hoogstraat 1) is number one among Antwerpenaars is not for its location, but for the fact that it's arguably the best frituur, or chip shop, in Antwerp.

Long-term owner Maria is a bit of an Antwerp character, famous for her banter with customers. And her chips are immaculate: double fried to perfection (the second fry to order), crisp on the outside, white and fluffy within.

At present, the chip shop looks much like any other, with a long counter and back-wall menu of portion sizes and sauces. But Maria has just bought the premises next door, has installed a seating area where you can take your wrap of chips and eat in comfort. Never the same as munching them in the street, mind.

young crowd who sip champagne and thick red wines. An attached delicatessen enables you to buy sun-dried tomatoes and olives in order to try and recreate it all at home. However, it seems daft to bother: why do your own when you can have the service wash?

Soep & Soup

89 Kammenstraat (03 707 28 05). **Meals served** 11am-6.30pm Mon-Sat. **Average** €. **No credit cards**.
Simple, this. Each day, Soep & Soup offers a choice of five soups in various sizes for eating in or taking out. That said, these are no ordinary soups: in the past, we've sampled such extravagances as a meal-size Italian minestrone with mushroom ravioli, chicken and parmesan croûtons, all served with hunks of wholemeal bread. Scrawled along the back wall of this stylish operation is the legend: 'In this bowl you may know heaven'. A bold statement (it actually comes from Molière), but not altogether far from the truth. Its location in the heart of the fashion district draws tons of trendies.

Sombat Thai Cuisine

1 Vleeshuisstraat (03 226 61 90). **Meals served** noon-2.30pm, 6-10.30pm Tue-Fri; 6-11pm Sat, Sun. **Average** €€€. **Credit** AmEx, MC, V.
Owner Sombat opened Les Larmes du Tigre in Brussels (*see p140*) before moving to Antwerp and setting up this big restaurant in the shadow of the Gothic Butcher's Hall. The food here has an authentic individuality about it, the usual lemongrass and ginger flavours being offset with sharp herbs such as Thai basil. Mixed dishes are quite the thing here: on one plate, you could tuck into satay,

small spring rolls, minced pork in banana leaves and fine, crispy noodles, all with dipping sauces and dainty condiments. It's a fine place, well worth a visit if you like Thai food but want to break away from the run-of-the-mill standard Westernised Thai menus.

El Warda

4 Draakstraat (03 239 31 13). **Meals served** 6-11pm Tue-Sun. **Average €. No credit cards**.
Small, cheap, informal and irresistibly Moroccan, El Warda will either set you up or finish you off with its traditional specialities. It's located near the drinking haven of Dageraadplats, an enclave of boozing spots where bar-hopping is a necessary pastime. It's a cosy place, and doesn't rub the magic lantern and Bedouin tent themes in your face too much. The menu is safe: tajines, couscous and the slightly more upmarket duck with dates. But Fatima Marzouki knows what she is doing and tries to bring something different to the table as the seasons swing. Certainly, pigeon tajine with almonds and honey is really something to write a postcard home about.

Wok a Way

14 Groendalstraat (03 213 13 13). **Meals served** 11.30am-8pm Mon-Sat. **Average €. No credit cards**.
Sophisticated fast food, anyone? Wok a Way is located in the middle of the town's main pedestrianised shopping area, and as such appeals to folk who need to drop their bags for a bit. However, it also draws crowds of thirtysomething professionals, attracted by the starkly minimalist decor, electric blue lighting and sushi conveyor belt, who want to pick up a packed lunch or take something home at the end of the day. The menu is described in quaintly hip English, taking in the unlikely likes of Flaming Lips soup, Let it Roll!! vegetarian dim sum, Seafood Slammers and Yankee Noodle stir-fries; sushi set menus round it all off.

The **Foreigner's Market** (Oude Vaartplaats, 8am-4pm Sat) sells food from around the Mediterranean in a colourful atmosphere. Among the delights are olives, cheeses, pastas, antipasti and tzatziki.

Bars

An Sibhin

44 Nationalestraat (03 226 72 51). **Open** 11am-late daily. **No credit cards**.
Though Antwerp has been blighted by Irish pubs that range from the average to the mediocre, the An Sibhin shines through for its blindingly simple role as a friendly place in which folks can drink and natter. No dreadful 'friends are strangers you're yet to meet' stickers, no shabby shillelaghs, no signposts for remote rural Irish towns, just standard drinks served with a smile – likewise

the pub food – to locals both native and expatriate in a homely ambience, heightened occasionally by Premiership action beamed in on Sky TV.

The Bar Room

30 Leopold de Waelplaats (03 257 57 40). **Open** 11am-2am daily. **Credit** AmEx, MC, V.

This cute and curvy two-floor DJ bar opposite the Fine Arts Museum is perfectly situated to attract the most musically discerning of the young trendies hanging out in 't Zuid; while older jazzers head for the Hopper (*see p201*) and pseuds prefer the ethnic binging and bonging of the Mogador (*see p204*), real beat buffs make a beeline for the Bar Room. Consisting of a small counter connected to a luxurious chill-out corner by a translucent walkway lined with weird little engines and DJ decks, the Bar Room's big plus is its downstairs parlour. Red drapes, as if dreamed up for the dancing dwarf in *Twin Peaks*, provide a suitable backdrop for foxy chatter over the sounds. Cocktails cost €6.30/€7.50.

Bar Tabac

43 Waalsekaai (03 238 19 37). **Open** *June-Sept* 7pm-late Mon-Thur; 4pm-late Fri; 1pm-late Sat, Sun. *Oct-May* 8pm-late Tue-Sat; 9pm-late Sun. **No credit cards**.

If any place has earned 't Zuid its reputation, it's the Bar Tabac. An after-hours haunt of fashionistas and the film community, the BT doesn't really start to shake its tail until gone midnight, when a superb soundtrack (Madonna to Serge Gainsbourg and most points in between) complements an atmosphere rarely more than two notches from cool. If you've had an evening of standard drinking in designer bars indistinct from any others in this corner of Europe and were wondering exactly why Antwerp is hyped to the nines, breeze into the Bar Tabac, particularly on a Sunday night, and all will become clear.

Bar 2

19 Vrijdagmarkt (03 227 54 36). **Open** 10am-2am Tue-Thur, Sat; 8am-late Fri; noon-8pm Sun. **No credit cards**.

The best joint on the busy, bar-blessed downtown square of Vrijdagmarkt, especially since the sad demise of the Elephant's Graveyard. Bar 2 attracts a more mixed crowd than the gay cycling community that haunts De Fiets, and a more discerning one than the Atlas II opposite. The simple, stylish interior provides a quiet backdrop for the busy lunchtime and evening bustle, fuelled by classy tapas, light snacks, English breakfasts and a wise selection of bottled beers. Oh yes, and the best Margaritas in town. In summer, it comes into its own, terrace tables jutting out on to the market square.

Regarded as the best bakers in Antwerp, **Goossens** (Korte Gasthuisstraat 31) has been kneading the dough for a century.

Berlin

1-3 Kleine Markt (03 227 11 01). **Open** 7.30am-late
Mon-Fri; 10am-late Sat, Sun. **Credit** AmEx, MC, V.
Vinko strikes again! After the success of Hangar 41, Bar
Italia and the Café Zürich, the local entrepreneur has
opened another in a similar vein (vain?), of elaborate
interior design and trendy wait staff: Berlin. (Somewhere
in the world, there must be a thin *Choose A Name For
Your Bar* book. Zanzibar, Bar Havana or Bar Moskva,
anyone?) The decor's black tiles, high ceilings, pinprick
spotlights and industrial-style air-conditioning, the
service on the snobby side of trendy. It opens for
breakfast and does a good trade for lunch, but by the
evening, it's mobbed. The menu caters for all times of day
and types of hunger, ranging from sandwiches and tapas
to three-course meals, including manifold veggie options.
At the back is a playroom, so parents can get laced on €6
Margaritas while junior does battle with the sticklebricks.

Den Billekletser

22 Hoogstraat (03 231 34 48). **Open** *Summer* 10am-late
daily. *Winter* 11am-late daily; closed Mon in Jan & Feb.
No credit cards.
A quirky bar packed with young drinkers vying to
outsmoke each other. During the day it's more bearable,
the upside-down globe, painting of a much-loved landlord
and brazen use of bric-a-brac creating the attractive
feeling you might get while enjoying a quiet pint at a
village auction. The locals veer towards the eccentric end
of the alternative set, some making the unwise decision
of bringing their dog in on the act. If it gets a bit much –
and you really can't swing a dog in here of a Saturday
night, however much you'd like to – then next door's
Pelican Dream is an oasis of conspiratorial bar natter.

Café Beveren

2 Vlasmarkt (03 231 22 25). **Open** 12.30pm-late Mon,
Thur-Sat; 1pm-late Sun. **No credit cards**.
Roll up, roll up! Step this way for the only fully working
De Cap fairground organ in all Antwerp, an old Rowe Ami
jukebox and a cast of dog-eared locals happy to tell you
their life stories while Gene Pitney wails a pitiless *24
Hours From Tulsa*. This is yer actual dockside Antwerp,
the kind of spot you might find in Rotterdam or Hamburg,
except that the good-time Johnnies, steamboat Willies and
long-suffering sweethearts have mellowed with age,
fumbling with their reading glasses before another round
of cards. The red-lined banquettes and spontaneous
outbreaks of old-time dancing encase the Beveren in a
lost era, a thousand shore-leave drink-ups pickled and
preserved for public consumption. Now in dry dock, the
Beveren can rest on its laurels, and allow the organ and
its listeners well-earned respite from the daily grind.

Antwerp

Het Elfde Gebod.
See p198.

Cappuccino Club

13 Sint-Laureiskaai (no phone). **Open** *May-Aug* noon-
4am daily. *Sept-Apr* 6pm-4am Tue-Sat. **No credit cards**.
Wily entrepreneurs are eschewing the easy but finite
pickings of the boomtown quays to the south for the
unchartered territory of the old docks and warehouses
in the north: 't Eilandje. And few places are better
positioned – knowingly but not annoyingly hip,
overlooking the steady lap of Napoleon's Bonaparte
Dock – than the Cappuccino Club. Tatty out and in, the
CC is saved by clever touches of design – an Italian menu
running over wall and ceiling, a mirror ball throwing
candlelight in patterns over the well stocked bar –
making it worth the modest trek north. Judicious use of
the teetering library of CDs keeps bums on tatty seats for
at least three drinks, to say nothing of the heady feeling
of sitting on the dock of a bay about to boom.

There's a
small market
with an
organic farm
stall and
fantastic
flowers on
**Dageraad-
plaats** each
week (9am-
1pm Thur).

Antwerp

De Duifkens

5 Graanmarkt (03 225 10 39). **Open** 11am-late Mon,
Tue, Thur, Fri; 10am-late Sat; 10am-9pm Sun. **No
credit cards**.

Set in the theatre district of Antwerp's Quartier Latin,
in a pleasant gabled square that hosts a thriving
Sunday-morning market called the Vogelenmarkt, De
Duifkens accommodates the local acting fraternity with
a homely, ageless wooden interior lined with portraits
of bygone stars of stage and screen. Where better to
tether your reputation, relax and imbibe between jobs?
The fireplace, dinky lights and sympathetic drone of
Antwaarps dialect at leisure engender a fiercely loyal
core of regulars, who prefer De Duifkens to the loud
banter of the commendably ornate Oud Arsenaal
around the corner. A handful of unusual beers tucked
behind the bar counter, too.

Antwerp

Het Elfde Gebod

10 Torfbrug (03 289 34 66). **Open** noon-1am Mon-Fri;
noon-2am Sat, Sun. **Credit** AmEx, MC, V.

Tourists like a talking point, a relief from a day's passive
gawping, lifeless chatter and bland nourishment. This
one is constructed in bas-relief, a façade of faux-medieval
sculptures of saints, angels and various religious bods
bowing in recognition of service to the tourist industry,
within touching distance of the north wing of the
Cathedral of Our Lady. Calling it a tourist trap would be
doing it an injustice: the statues have been here for a
century, the tables are hulkingly authentic wooden
affairs, there are usually at least 30 different beers in
stock, and other nice touches include a homage to
turncoat atheist Diderot in the back area. The name, too,

High times in Flanders

It is, after all, the national drink
of Flanders. So it seems only
appropriate that the history of
genever should be as colourful
as that of Flanders itself.
Favoured by British soldiers
fighting in Flanders fields in the
1500s, 'Dutch Courage' was
taken across the Channel and
adapted as plain old gin.

Back to the real McCoy,
though, whose own origins date
back to the pre-Plague days
when medieval alchemists
brewed DIY digestives from
boiled rainwater and juniper
berries. Switching to distilled
water when the Black Death
struck the Low Countries in the
14th century, the distillation
then became alcohol, in varying
forms and tastes. The most
palatable and popular was grain
brandy, occasionally flavoured
with juniper berries.

Even today, juniper is not
essential to genever ('jenever'
in Flemish). The Dutch were
keen to experiment with various

fruit flavours, frequent abolition
resulting in profitable brewers
upping stills and moving
operations to nearby northern
France and western Germany.
When it was legal to produce
the drink, there was still no law
to control its strength or the mix
of ingredients.

With the industrialisation
of Belgium in the early 19th
century, this maverick approach
became a huge social problem.
Cheap, industrial alcohol –
using such raw materials as
sugar beet and molasses – was
befuddling and endangering the
working population. Locals were
downing the stuff not because
of its taste – the grainy flavour
had all but disappeared – but
to stupify themselves at either
end of the working day. Belgium
was drowning in railroad gin.

Invading German troops
confiscated all copper stills
in 1914, and a year after the
war came the Vandervelde Law
that banned or, in other cases,

Antwerp

is nothing new; there are 11th Commandment bars all over the Netherlands, including a decent example of the breed in Amsterdam's Red Light District.

Den Engel

5 Grote Markt (03 233 12 52). **Open** 9am-late daily.
No credit cards.

Antwerp's bar of all bars. It isn't fab or fashionable, and whatever edges it once cut blunted long ago; it is simply an institution for those who can't face to be in one right now. This ramshackle pub provides welcome relief from the officialdom next door at the Town Hall. Councillors clink glasses with nervous fiancés, journalists accept drinks and gossip from politicians, while locals of all ages provide a cheery backdrop. Part of the furniture – literally – is Ronny Meyers, a toothless octogenarian

severely limited sales of strong spirits. In any case, the drink had earned itself a scuzzy reputation. Even when available on the black market, genever had fallen out of fashion.

As customs – and Customs and Excise – relaxed, genever sales slowly picked up in the 1970s, although it wasn't until 1984 (!) that the prohibition law of 1919 was repealed. Almost at once, as if asserting national pride (and catching up with the Dutch, whose own tasting houses, proeflokalen, dot the dark alleyways of Amsterdam), genever bottles again lined the bar shelves of Flanders. Most famously, **De Vagant** (*see p207*) collated a stock of some 200 varieties in downtown Antwerp, complementing them with a drinks menu documenting the qualities of each. Fruit genevers were also produced in bulk and, lower in alcohol, are now the most popular type.

With fashionable bars extolling its virtues, genever gradually lost its old soak image, and began to be appreciated across the board. Chefs prepared fine meals with it and arguments raged over origins and qualities. Unsurprisingly, the Dutch and Belgians each claimed historic ownership. Antwerp is considered one source, though Hasselt in East Flanders boasts both the **National Genever Museum** (Witte Nonnenstraat 19, 011 24 11 44, www.jenevermuseum.be) and Belgium's biggest distillery, Smeets.

Responsible for the famous brand Extra Smeets, the company is one of only nine producers who distil what is considered authentic Belgian genever; Bruggeman's Hertekamp and Peterman, and Filliers' Oude Graanjenever are other prominent brands to lure the initiated and the curious.

pictured holding a Bolleke bigger than himself. Faded De Koninck campaigns, pre-war school photos, officers' hats and the charted bankability of the regulars' holiday savings accounts vie for attention. The Angel will be observing the daily deeds of Antwerp long after every fad has faded, outlasting the neighbouring bar which copes with its overflow. It's called Den Bengel, or 'The Miscreant'; good against evil, as ever was in Antwerp's historic heart.

Entrepôt du Congo

42 Vlaamsekaai (03 257 16 48). **Open** 8am-3am Mon-Fri; 8am-4am Sat, Sun. **No credit cards.**

This pioneering enterprise began the regeneration of the southern quaysides – 't Zuid – into the trendy quarter of galleries and designer bars it is today. A century ago, Congo boats would dock here, unloading crates of colonial plunder into this grand corner edifice. A century later, it accommodates the post-colonial generation, and not without irony. A classy, bare wood-and-floortile interior displays only one deference to decoration: a framed portrait of King Baudouin in postage-stamp humour over the bar. The place is still justifiably popular, despite a plethora of competition an anchor-toss away, although the bar food might have something to do with it.

De Faam

12 Grote Pieter Potstraat (03 234 05 78). **Open** 4pm-4am daily. **No credit cards.**

In a street packed with bars, modest De Faam stands head and shoulders above the rest. With its long bar counter, low lighting and louche choice of music, it's a tasteful place, but one that succeeds in attracting a romantic crowd without appearing to make any effort so to do. Cornered into quick description, it would be easy to reach for 'cosy' and 'sophisticated', but De Faam defies easy platitudes. It's simply a good bar, well run and well supported. Alongside, the disco lights of De Vuile Was ('Dirty Laundry') seem positively rudimentary.

Fuga

15-17 Nassaustraat (03 231 31 58/www.restofuga.be). **Open** 11am-2am Mon-Fri; 6pm-late Sat, Sun. **Credit** MC, V.

A bright venture in the dark docklands, the extravagant Fuga, the smartest bar on 't Eilandje, will sink or swim depending on how quickly this yet-to-be-exploited enclave sprouts peers. Comprising a restaurant and a lounge bar, the latter a narrow strip of bar-counter, moulded plastic chairs and colours seemingly picked from a packet of Refreshers, the Fuga would clean up in a south- or quayside location. But although busy of a Saturday, the Fuga can be deathly quiet when little else

Hopper

Antwerp

stirs amid the docks. An attractive selection of cocktails,
DJs five nights of the week and the Metropole taxi depot
next door work in its favour.

Hopper

2 Leopold de Waelstraat (03 248 49 33). **Open** 10.30am-
late daily. **No credit cards**.
Coolly propping up a corner between the Fine Arts
Museum and the river, the Hopper calmly established
itself as the most prestigious jazz venue in town before
expanding its repertoire to embrace its now widely
acknowledged status as Best Bar on the Block. Possibly
maybe. In any case, on jazz-free nights (Thursday to
Sunday, and every evening in July and August), it's
packed with older trendies talking fads, fashion and other
fripperies; anything but the gritty stuff silently
contemplated by Edward's historic, iconic diner
nighthawks. Picture windows, a crazee painting above
the bar and glossy mags shown off over the house piano
confect further ambience, in the unlikely event any
further confection were needed.

Kapitein Zeppos

78 Vleminckveld (03 231 17 89). **Open** 10am-late
Mon-Fri; 11am-late Sat, Sun. **No credit cards**.
Kapitein Zeppos, a popular detective on children's TV,
provides a reasonable device for a theme for this classy
bar set between the centre and 't Zuid. Zeppos, via a big
portrait, presides over a well-run operation that attracts
a trendy, generally coupled-up clientele here equally for
the bites (soups, salads and sandwiches) and the beer.
The decor takes in books, plants, old radios and a stucco
ceiling, but if it all gets too twee, the atmospheric wooden
De Pallieter diagonally opposite beckons the theatrical
fraternity and bachelors both lonely and predatory.

Kleine Bourla

3 Kelderstraat (03 232 16 32). **Open** 11am-late Mon-Sat.
Credit AmEx, DC, MC, V.
Built by Pierre Bruno Bourla at the time of Belgian
independence, the splendidly restored Bourla Theatre is
served by two fancy cafés: the ornate De Foyer on the
first floor, and the Kleine Bourla next door. Both do
justice to the artistic surroundings, and operate as entities
separate to the theatre. The Kleine Bourla bistro boasts
a tasteful interior, with a life-size harlequin set against a
background of stunning red. A popular spot in which the
literary and theatre sets gather for power elevenses and
afternoon teas, it also serves main meals – salads and the
like – that are best enjoyed on its terrace in summer.

Kulminator

32 Vleminckveld (03 232 45 38). **Open** 8pm-midnight
Mon; 11am-midnight Tue; 5pm-midnight Wed, Thur; 5pm-
1am Fri, Sat. **No credit cards**.
Tagged by some sources as 'the best bar in Antwerp', the
Kulminator isn't. However, it does hold a special place in
the heart of the discerning cosmopolitan barhopper.
Why? Well, 500 beers, for a start, collated in row upon
row of colourful labels, temptingly stored in full view of
all squeezing to the toilets. As well as all sorts of goodies
on draught, there are beers of the month and praise in
scribbled hyperbole by learned imbibers from Grimsby
to St Petersburg in the weighty visitors' book. Locals use
the venue for special occasions, smoke and candlelight
flickering over the obligatory old posters and invasive
arbour. A tight fit, but not without reward.

Moeskop

17 Dageraadplaats (03 272 10 80). **Open** 11.55am-2am
Mon-Fri; 2.55pm-2am Sun. **No credit cards**.
A small corner bar that can claim to have regenerated the
Zurenborg enclave of artists and intellectuals the other
side of the Diamond Quarter from Centraal Station. As a

**Philip's
Biscuits**
(Korte
Gasthuisstraat
11) offers the
most sublime
spéculoos,
macaroons
and marzipan.
Check out the
window for
a nostalgic
display of
gingerbread-
house
memories.

Kleine Bourla. *See p202.*

grocer's, its surroundings were anonymous; as a biker's bar, they gained a personality, albeit an ugly one. In the mid-1990s, a genial Dutch barman transformed the modest space into a laid-back bar of rare character, thanks to a fine selection of beers (Westmalle on tap!), discerning music and unusual decor (glitter mosaic spreads on the walls, stern old portraits, a framed Dutch dictionary definition of 'Moeskoepper', which ordinarily translates either as 'sulky person' or 'poacher' but here is a play on the surname of proprietor Adriaan Moeskops). Zurenborg being Zurenborg, the 'village within a town', all sorts drift through the door, except during the unusual closing times of Saturday night and New Year's Eve. Home-made soups are a speciality, 'ecological soap of the week' a peculiarity.

Mogador

57 Graaf van Egmontstraat (03 238 71 60).
Open 5pm-late daily. **Credit** AmEx, MC, V.
Named after a place in Morocco, the improbably popular Mogador comprises an übertrendy grouping of low-black seating and minimalist decor packed with incessantly chattering locals delighted to know they're supping on the flavour of the month of Antwerp bars. Give it another few weeks and most will have moved on, but for now they enjoy ringing a bell to gain entry through a hefty iron door, slinking down next to fellow fashionistas, and wantonly ignoring the bowls of delicate snacks that arrive with each expensive beer. With Corona at €4 a pop, you're as well ordering a €7 dry Martini, or a €7.5 glass of Piper Heidsieck champagne. Extras: terrace in summer, frequent DJs, prime Fine Arts Museum location.

De Muze

15 Melkmarkt (03 226 01 26). **Open** noon-4am daily.
No credit cards.
In the 1960s, De Muze was Antwerp's little Amsterdam, a bar for bums and beatniks gathered around the glow of the gigglestick. Some are still here, but some were missing in the 1990s, when the bar acquired a serious revamp, keeping much of its original spirit (smoke excepted). Just as important as a live music venue – jazz these days, with pleasingly little recourse for hour-long guitar solos – De Muze still displays a curious set of collages and an even stranger horse-cum-motorbike mobile contraption dangling before a now confusing warren of floor levels. Despite the guaranteed aural backdrop of at least three versions of *My Funny Valentine*, the ambience is neither miserable nor muso; De Muze has grown old gracefully. Good bar food, too.

De Nieuwe Linde

49 Pacificatiestraat (03 248 14 86). **Open** 5pm-late daily.
No credit cards.

Set back in the dark hinterland behind the focal Fine Arts Museum, the New Litten Tree provides the underground literary and artistic community with a grungy gathering place out of sight from the fierce spotlight of recognition in the prominent bars on the nearby main drags of Waalsekaai, Vlaamsekaai and Leopold de Waelplaats. Budding Bukowskis can philander with impunity by low candlelight, underneath the obligatory incongruous chandeliers and esoteric portraits. The corrugated iron bar counter contributes to the squat ambience, though the earthiness is counterbalanced by the high ceiling and delicate choice of music.

't Oerwoud

2 Suikerrui (03 233 14 12). **Open** noon-late daily.
Credit AmEx, MC, V.
A step back from the quayside, two steps from the brazen tourism of the town centre and opposite the medieval fortress of the Steen, the ship shape of 't Oerwoud marks the corner of Suikerrui and Jordaenskaai. The Jungle is a relaxing lunch spot – salads, soups and pastas, with many dishes served until very late – but mostly serves as a busy pre-club livener. Spotlights blaze over the curved bar, speakers boom with popular dance sounds, and the nachos machine and upholstered leather seating of the chill-and-chat back area soon become buried in a fog of Bastos. Cocktails at €6.25 keep the party atmosphere rampant until the youngish crowd head for the bright lights of the nearby docks.

Old Trafford

5 Leopoldplaats (03 290 76 56). **Open** 10am-8pm daily.
No credit cards.
It's not a particularly edifying establishment, nor is it even a brilliant bar in a city with 500 of them, yet the Old Trafford is surely the only one in the whole of Flanders dedicated to Manchester United. Here, you can order beans on toast and Walker's crisps, while *Glory Glory Man United* booms from the speakers and Sky Sports plays on TV. Whether you cherish it or remain churlish, the Old Trafford at least serves the dutiful game in a city woefully bereft (Royal Antwerp FC last crowned champions in 1957!) of football culture. Local and adopted team shots adorn the walls; note that RAFC are one of a handful of clubs with whom United share a nursery arrangement.

De Pelikaan

14 Melkmarkt (03 227 23 51). **Open** 9am-late daily.
No credit cards.
Soon to celebrate its 50th anniversary, the downtown, downbeat Pelican has been dragging writers, designers and musicians through its doors and keeping them glued to its bar counter for longer than most care to remember.

Zuiderterras. See p208.

Located in the shadow of the cathedral, it makes no effort to appeal to curious passers-by, leaving all the dressing-up to more malleable establishments nearby. For that matter, it isn't even dressed down: it's just got out of bed and put on whatever it could find on the bedroom floor, invariably the same as what it found there yesterday. Enter, drink, swap stories, get drunk, go home. Perfect.

Popi

22 Riemstraat (03 238 15 30). **Open** *Summer* 5pm-late Tue-Sat; 4pm-late Sun. *Winter* 6pm-late Tue-Sat; 4pm-late Sun. **No credit cards**.

This popular gay and lesbian bar close to 't Zuid was impossibly mobbed during its anniversary celebrations in the run-up to Christmas 2002, but it's never really all that quiet. Brash, cheeky (its name refers to the Russian for backside) and a martyr to its Abba obsession, Popi

 Dockside dining

The best · Dockside dining

Chez Fl'Eau
Modern classics. *See p169.*

't Fornuis
Reach for the (Michelin) stars. *See p173.*

Het Pomphuis
A pump-house no more. *See p191.*

doesn't take itself in the least bit seriously, a relief amid the venues nearby, filled with a po-faced crowd staring into its coffee. Four years young, Popi has still got a lot of living to do. Yet if it gets too much, the traditional old Vismijn bar next door is a welcome port in a storm.

De Scène
2 Graaf van Hoornestraat (03 238 64 42). **Open** 4pm-3am Mon-Wed, Sun; 4pm-5am Thur-Sat. **No credit cards**.
A happening destination bar in 't Zuid, set on a corner by the Fine Arts Museum, where studiously hip trendies gather and gas beneath a strange, sunbeam-surfaced globe. Musicians and DJs flock here in their dozens to hear weekend spinners such as DJ Joe Tattoo, a heavy name to drop in these parts. The drinks are in the usual range, but are served with swift aplomb by the kind of bar staff who practise and preach the religion of hair gel. A good place to find out what's going on in town, and hook up with whoever's going along there.

De Vagant
25 Reyndersstraat (03 233 15 38). **Open** 11am-late Mon-Sat; noon-late Sun. **No credit cards**.
Genever was to Antwerp what gin was to London, the opiate of historic port cities drowned in a sea of cheap alcohol. Sailors, dockers and dizzy damsels merrily drank for a franc and death-wish drank for two before a prohibition that lasted until 1984. This innocuous bar opened a year later, with 200 types of formerly forbidden genever in myriad strengths and flavours, accompanied by small chunks of cheese and deft slices of meat. Sipped and not slammed (spot the foreigner!), genever's potted history embellishes De Vagant's drinks menu and exquisite interior of old flagons and pre-prohibition posters. Upstairs, a restaurant serves dishes concocted from the stuff. Downstairs, a genial barman dispenses little else, honourably excepting Bolleke and chase-able lagers. Anything else would go against the grain.

Antwerp

Het Zand

9 Sint-Jansvliet (03 232 56 67). **Open** 11am-late daily.
No credit cards.
Located just by the grand entrance of the St Anna foot
tunnel, the Sand displays the calculating hand of the
Celtic fraternity. Yet despite the fading promise of a
peeling 'Guinness Gift Shop' sign, this is essentially
a hostelry in the classic Antwerp tradition. Although a
decade of Irish management has seen a permanent
fixture of Kilkenny bunting and Irish stew, Het Zand is
as close as you've ever likely to get to sitting in a pre-war
Antwerp living room with a bar attached. Wooden tables
heave under heavy lunches, old geezers prop up the tall
brick bar getting stotious to Deano, while the unusual
local tradition of displaying death masks of regulars
passed on is upheld overhead. Above, the creaky
furniture of the live-in ownership completes the picture
of boozy homestead.

Zeezicht

7-8 Dageraadplaats (03 235 10 65). **Open** 11.30am-late
Mon-Fri; noon-late Sat, Sun. **No credit cards**.
The most prominent of the venues profiting from the rise
in fortunes of the formerly desolate Zurenborg district, the
Sea View is a spacious corner bar with a dining section
that slips easily into something cooler as lunchtime fades
into boozy eve. Tapas are available for either, but the
square bar is invariably lined with serious hedonists at
various stages of one-way missions to Planet Blotto. This
is not to say, though, that the Zeezicht is threatening. Far
from it: turtlenecked intellectuals pose for hours at a time
at its picture windows for the supposed benefit of the
substantial female clientele, all to the disapproval of the
vast propagandist image of Lenin that peers down from
the back wall.

Zuiderterras

37 Ernest van Dijckkaai (03 234 12 75). **Open** 9am-
midnight daily. **Credit** AmEx, MC, V.
Straddling the promenade that lines the Schelde just
before it does a dramatic estuary dive into the North
Sea, the South Terrace is a ship-shaped, sheeny-interiored
Bob van Reeth creation. The sleek two-floor operation
centres on a circular bar counter serviced by the quick
flitting of a smart wait staff, whose abrupt efficiency
doesn't begin to dent the romantic mood of the twinkling
Scheldt at sundown. On weekend lunchtimes, the media
and design set interrupt work-related conversation and
gossip in order to accommodate the annoyingly
perceptive attentions of their offspring, drowning out
foghorns in the din. It's pricey, sure, but potentially a
weekend highlight.

Glossary

General terminology

French	English	Flemish
un couteau	**knife**	mes
une fourchette	**fork**	vork
une cuillère	**spoon**	lepel
une serviette	**napkin**	serviette
le sel	**salt**	zout
le poivre	**pepper**	peper
du pain	**bread**	brood
du beurre	**butter**	boter
au fût	**on draught**	van 't vat
une bouteille	**bottle**	fles
un cendrier	**ashtray**	asbak
fumeur/non fumeur	**smoking/ non-smoking**	rokers/ niet rokers
végétarien(ne)	**vegetarian**	vegetarisch

Glossary

l'addition	**the bill**	de rekening
un reçu	**receipt**	rekening
bancontact	**local debit card**	bancontact
carte bancaire	**credit card**	credit card
du liquide	**cash**	cash
un pourboire	**tip**	drinkgeld

Menu basics

apéritif	**aperitif**	aperitief
pour commencer	**to begin with**	om te beginnen
chaud	**warm/hot**	warm
froid	**cold**	koud
entrées chaudes	**warm starters**	warme voorgerechten
entrées froides	**cold starters**	koude voorgerechten
potages	**soups**	soepen
plats	**main courses**	hoofdschotels
moules	**mussels**	mosselen
viandes	**meat dishes**	vleesgerechten
poissons	**fish dishes**	visgerechten
fromages	**cheeses**	kazen
desserts	**desserts**	nagerechten/ desserts
spécialités	**daily specials**	suggesties
plat du jour	**cheap daily special**	dagschotel/ dagmenu
service/TVA compris	**service and sales tax included**	dienst en BTW inbegrepen

Common phrases

comme boisson?	**what would you like to drink?**	war wilt u drinken?
c'est chaud	**be careful – the plate's hot**	opgelet – het bord is warm
bon appétit	**enjoy your meal**	smakelijk
s'il vous plâit	**to attract attention**	alstublieft

Cooking terms

cru	**raw**	rauw
farci(e)	**stuffed**	gevuld
au four	**in the oven**	in de oven
fumé	**smoked**	gerookt
glacé(e)	**iced**	bevrozen
gratiné(e)	**with melted cheese or breadcrumbs**	gegratineerd
grillé(e)	**grilled**	gegrild
haché	**minced**	gehakt
mariné(e)	**marinated**	gemarineerd

Glossary

au naturel	**plainly cooked**	gekookt
en papillote	**baked in foil or paper**	en papillote
purée	**mashed**	puree
rôti	**roasted**	gebraden
sauté(e)	**shallow fried**	gesauteerd
à la vapeur	**steamed**	gestoomd
Quelle cuisson?	**How would you like it cooked?**	Hoe wenst u het gebakken?

• *Beef*

bleu	**virtually raw**	bleu
saignant	**rare**	saignant
à point	**medium rare**	à point
bien cuit	**well cooked**	bien cuit/ doorbakken

• *Lamb, duck, kidneys, liver*

| rosé | **medium rare** | rosé |

Viande/meat/vlees

agneau	**lamb**	lam
boeuf	**beef**	rund
boudin noir/ blanc	**black/white pudding**	zwarte/witte beuling
canard	**duck**	eend
cervelle	**brain**	hersenen
chevreuil	**venison**	ree/reebok
dinde	**turkey**	kalkoen
escargot de Bourgogne	**snail**	wijngaardslak
faisan	**pheasant**	fazant
foie	**liver**	lever
gibier	**game**	wild
cuisses de grenouille	**frog's legs**	kikkerbillen
jambon	**ham**	hesp
lapin	**rabbit**	konijn
lard	**bacon**	spek
lièvre	**hare**	haas
porc	**pork**	varken
poulet	**chicken**	kip
rognon	**kidney**	nier
sanglier	**boar**	everzwijn
saucisse	**sausage**	worst
veau	**veal**	kalf
volaille	**poultry/chicken**	gevogelte

Poisson & fruits de mer/ fish & seafood/vis & schaaldieren

crustacé	**shellfish**	schaaldier
anguille	**eel**	paling
cabillaud	**cod**	kabeljauw

carrelet	**plaice**	schol
crevette	**shrimp**	garnaal
daurade	**sea bream**	goudbrasem
églefin	**haddock**	schelvis
espadon	**swordfish**	zwaardvis
hareng	**herring**	haring
homard	**lobster**	kreeft
huître	**oyster**	oester
langoustine	**Dublin Bay prawn/scampi**	langoustine/ Noorse kreeft
maquereau	**mackerel**	makreel
morue	**cod**	kabeljauw
moule	**mussel**	mossel
raie	**skate**	rog
saumon	**salmon**	zalm
seiche	**squid**	inktvis
truite	**trout**	forel

Légumes/vegetables/groenten

ail	**garlic**	look
artichaut	**artichoke**	artisjok
asperge	**asparagus**	asperge
champignon	**mushroom**	champignon
chicon	**chicory/ Belgian endive**	witloof
chou	**cabbage**	kool
chou-fleur	**cauliflower**	bloemkool
épinards	**spinach**	spinazie
haricot	**bean**	boon
haricot vert	**French bean**	prinsesseboon
oignon	**onion**	ui/ajuin
poireau	**leek**	prei
poivron vert/ rouge	**green/red pepper**	groene/rode peper
pomme de terre	**potato**	aardappel/patat
truffe	**truffle**	truffel

Fruits/fruit/fruit

ananas	**pineapple**	ananas
banane	**banana**	banaan
cassis	**blackcurrant**	zwarte bes
cerise	**cherry**	kers
citron	**lemon**	citroen
citron vert	**lime**	limoen
fraise	**strawberry**	aardbei
framboise	**raspberry**	framboos
pamplemousse	**grapefruit**	pompelmoes
pêche	**peach**	perzik
poire	**pear**	peer
pomme	**apple**	appel
prune	**plum**	pruim
raisin	**grape/raisin**	druif/rozijn

Desserts/desserts/ nagerechten or desserten

crème Chantilly	**whipped cream**	slagroom
crème fouettée	**whipped cream**	slagroom
crème glacée	**ice-cream**	roomijs
gâteau	**cake**	cake
glace	**ice**	ijs
glacé/glacée	**frozen or iced**	bevrozen

Other foodstuffs

frites	**chips**	frieten
fromage	**cheese**	kaas
miel	**honey**	honing
moutarde	**mustard**	mosterd
noix	**walnut**	walmoot
oeuf	**egg**	ei
pâtes	**pasta**	pasta
potage	**soup**	soep
riz	**rice**	rijst
sucre	**sugar**	suiker

Drinks

de l'eau	**water**	water
vin blanc	**white wine**	witte wijn
vin rouge	**red wine**	rode wijn
jus d'orange	**orange juice**	sinaasappelsap
une bière	**draught beer**	bier/pint
café	**regular coffee**	koffie
thé	**tea**	thee

Belgian specialities

andouillette
A sausage made from chitterlings, left-over bits and offal, and graded with As for roughness (the toughest is AAAAA). Delicious with mustard sauce.

anguilles au vert/paling in 't groen
Bite-size pieces of eel in a vivid green sauce of spinach, parsley and sorrel.

boudin/beuling
Another sausage, but in two varieties: the white version is made from minced chicken and/or pork, and bound with cream and egg, while the black version gets its colour from fresh blood.

carbonades flamandes/stoofvlees
Stewing steak, usually cooked slowly in dark Belgian beer. Some recipes involve gingerbread and laurel. The sauce is rich and heavy.

croquettes aux crevettes/garnaalkroketten
Deep-fried croquettes, often egg-shaped, filled with a sauce of tiny sweet North Sea shrimps.

filet américain
A variation of steak tartare: raw minced beef seasoned with shallots, mayonnaise and paprika. The cheaper variety is used in sandwiches; the real fillet is a main course.

fondues au fromage/kaaskroketten
Deep-fried croquettes filled with a thick cheesy sauce. Also known as 'fondue parmesan', to avoid confusion with the Swiss dipping variety.

jambon des Ardennes/ardeense ham
Smoked ham from the forest region of the Ardennes in the south-east of Belgium, made using juniper as an additional flavouring.

lapin à la Kriek/konijn in Kriek
Rabbit stewed in cherries and Kriek (cherry beer), giving a decent mix of sweet and sour.

moules/mosselen
The ubiquitous mussels. They come from the Zeeland coast, and are plump and plentiful. The basic recipe is marinières in stock with chopped vegetables and a lot of celery.

steak
On many Belgian menus, you will just see 'steak', a rump cut. Mix and match your sauces, from green peppercorn to a classic béarnaise.

stoemp
A mashed mix of potatoes and other vegetables. Some add minced meats, but the veggie variety is usually topped off with a sausage or ham.

tomate aux crevettes
A chunky beef tomato stuffed with mayonnaise and crevettes grises.

vol-au-vent
The familiar pastry case, but filled with chicken in a creamy sauce. If 'de poularde', it's a top quality, free-range fattened bird.

waterzooi
A stew is common throughout Belgium. Made with chicken and vegetables, it is enriched with cream and egg yolks, and must be made fresh.

Glossary

Index

Index

Index

Ad index

Please refer to the relevant pages for addresses and telephone numbers.

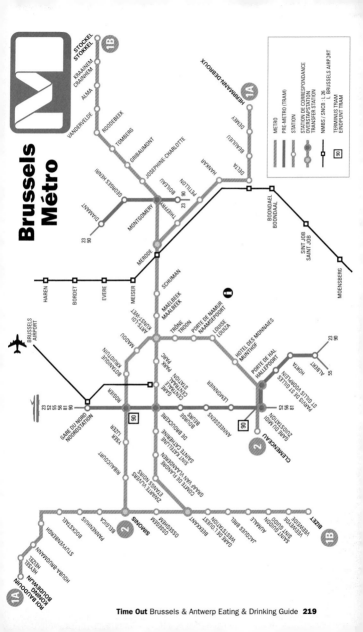

Brussels Métro

Legend

METRO
PRE-METRO (TRAM)
STATION
STATION DE CORRESPONDANCE
OVERSTAPSTATION
TRANSFER STATION
NMBS / SNCB · L.26
L · BRUSSELS AIRPORT
TERMINUS TRAM
EINDPUNT TRAM
90

Stations

STOCKEL STOKEL
KRAAINEM CRAINHEM
ALMA
VANDERVELDE
ROODEBEEK
TOMBERG
GRIBAUMONT
JOSEPHINE-CHARLOTTE
GEORGES HENRI
DIAMANT
MONTGOMERY
THIEFFRY
PETILLON
HANKAR
DELTA
BEAULIEU
DEMEY
HERRMANN-DEBROUX
MERODE
SCHUMAN
MAELBEEK MAALBEEK
ARTS-LOI KUNST-WET
TRONE TROON
PORTE DE NAMUR NAAMSEPOORT
LOUISE LOUIZA
HOTEL DES MONNAIES MUNTHOF
PORTE DE HAL HALLEPOORT
PARVIS DE ST GILLES ST-GILLIS VOORPLEIN
HORTA
ALBERT
HAREN
BORDET
EVERE
MEISER
MADOU
BOTANIQUE KRUIDTUIN
PARC PARK
GARE CENTRALE CENTRAAL STATION
ROGIER
BRUSSELS AIRPORT
GARE DU NORD NOORDSTATION
YSER IJZER
SAINT CATHERINE SINT KATELIJNE
DE BROUCKERE
BOURSE BEURS
ANNEESSENS
LEMONNIER
GARE DU MIDI ZUIDSTATION
CLEMENCEAU
BOONDAEL BOONDAAL
SINT JOB SAINT JOB
MOENSBERG
RIBAUCOURT
COMTE DE FLANDRE GRAAF VAN VLAANDEREN
ETANGS NOIRS ZWARTE VIJVERS
SAINTE CATHERINE SINT KATELIJNE
OSSEGHEM OSSEGEM
BEEKKANT
GARE DE L'OUEST WESTSTATION
BELGICA
PANNENHUIS
BOCKSTAEL
STUYVENBERGH
HOUBA-BRUGMANN
HEYSEL HEIZEL
ROI BAUDOUIN KONING BOUDEWIJN
SIMONIS
JACQUES BREL
AUMALE
SAINT GUIDON SINT GUIDO
VEEWEYDE
VEEWEYDE
BIZET

1A 1B 2

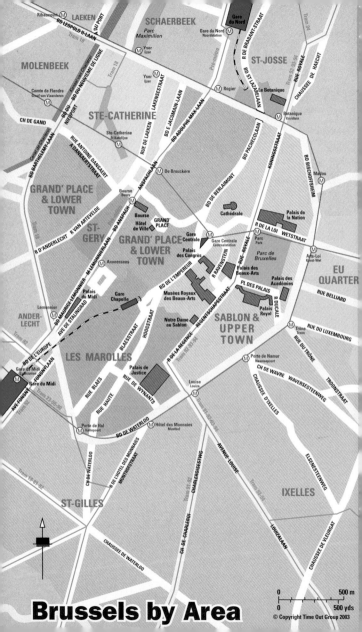

Brussels by Area